NINJA FOO

COOKBOOK

FOR BEGINNERS

550 Easy & Delicious Recipes to Air Fry, Pressure Cook, Dehydrate, and more

By

Carol Newman

DISCLAIMER

The information contained in this book is geared for educational and entertainment purposes only. Strenuous efforts have been made towards providing accurate, up to date and reliable complete information. The information in this book is true and

complete to the best of our knowledge. Neither the publisher nor the author takes

any responsibility for any possible consequences of reading or enjoying the recipes in

this book. The author and publisher disclaim any liability in connection with the use of information contained in this book. Under no circumstance will any legal

responsibility or blame be apportioned against the author or publisher for any reparation, damages, or monetary loss due to the information herein, either directly or indirectly.

Table of Contents

INTRODUCTION
Meaning of Ninja Foodi

This is a new trending kitchen appliance. It is a pressure cooker that crisps. Ninja has a 6.5qt pressure cooker along with a 4qt Cook & crisp basket for the Tender Crisp (this is an Air Fryer function). It is correct to say that the Ninja Foodi is an Air Fryer, a pressure cooker and a dehydrator. The appliance allows you to turn ingredients that are tough to become tender, juicy and full of flavor.

It cooks food as faster as you could expect. The Ninja Foodi is usually called and ultimate Air Fryer due to its crisping lid that is powerful. Ninja Foodi is a unit that uses super-heated steam to put moisture and flavor into your foods. The crisping lid releases hot air all around your food for a crispy result. The Ninja Foodi is a combination of 4 in 1 appliance which includes: A pressure cooker, dehydrator, slow cooker and air fryer.

Benefits of Using the Ninja Foodi:

There are lots of benefits you can get from using this appliance. The benefit that outweighs other appliances is that it does not require you to flip the fries over to the other side many times compared to other pressure cookers. You may only shake the fries on halfway to cooking time for a proper cooking. The benefits are shown below:

1. **Crispy Wings**

Start cooking your chicken or turkey wings even in haste with the pressure cooker mode. When the normal cooking is done, switch to the air fryer to get that hot air circulating all around the wings and gives you a crispy result. You can combine with any sauce of your choice for your dinner or as an appetizer.

2. **Baked Macaroni and Cheese**

This unit allows you to cook macaroni and cheese and gives you a crispy result. When you are done with the normal cooking, you can swap to the Air Fryer mode for that crispy golden-brown topping that you would get when baked.

3. **Scalloped Potatoes**

Everybody loves a eating creamy scalloped potatoes. The unit tenders your potatoes and then with the air fryer for a crispy result. Ninja Foodi allows you to cook all kinds of food unlike other units like air fryer or pressure cooker.

4. **Pressure cook and crisp**

Ninja Foodi enables you to pressure cook something and then make it crispy. This crispiness makes the chicken you cook not to require that you bring the chicken to the broiler. Everything can stay neat and nice.

Cooking things at once is very beneficial and helpful to Ninja Foodi users because it is not time-consuming cooking a healthy food with the unit. The parts are easy to clean and it has a large cooking capacity.

Function Keys of Your Ninja Foodi:

Ninja Foodi comes with many buttons for optimum operation of the unit which includes steam, slow cook, pressure cook, sear/sauté button, air crisp, broil, bake /roast and keep warm, buttons respectively. It also has buttons for temperature and time controls, start/stop button. The buttons and their functions are shown below:

1. **Pressure cook:**

This button helps you to cook your meal up to 4 hours using high or low pressure. As earlier said, it is possible to adjust the cooking time to 1-minute increment for 1 hour. When the time is up, you may increase the time to 5 minutes and begin to cook up to 4 hours. Hence you can make a whole lot of meals.

2. **Air Crisp:**

This function gives you an opportunity to adjust the temperature to either 300°F or 400°F and also adjust to increase the cooking time to 2 minutes for the highest cooking time of 1 hour. The air crisp button is used in cooking many dishes like chicken tenders, French fries etc. Pressure cooked food can be crisp using this button.

3. **Bake/Roast:**

This setting in the Ninja is good for making roasted meats and baked foods. For this function, the Ninja Foodi uses the air-frying lid. There is no problem if you set the cooking time to 1-minute increment for 1 hour. When the time is up, you may increase the time to 5 minutes and begin to cook up to 4 hours. After the hour mark, you can increase the time in five-minute increments and cook for up to four hours.

4. **Steam:**

It is possible to steam your veggies and other meals by putting the pressure lid on the Ninja Foodi with the sealing valve in the vent position.

5. **Slow cook:**

This button also makes use of the pressure lid with the sealing valve in the vent position. It is possible for you to slow cook low or slow cook high. The cooking time can also be adjusted to 15 minutes increment for up to 12 hours. It is advisable to use the slow cook mode when cooking meals like stews, soup or pot roasts.

6. **Sear/Sauté:**

This button on the Ninja Foodi does not make use of the lid. It only has a temperature setting of 5 different modes respectively. These includes: medium, medium-high, high, low or medium-low, setting. Foods can be browned after cooking or before cooking. The button can also be used to make different kinds of sauces, gravies. This button functions the same as you would sear or sauté using your stovetop.

Ninja Foodi Pressure Releasing Methods:

This process is ideal for stopping all cooking process in order to avoid the food getting burnt. Foods like corn or broccoli etc. are ideal for this pressure releasing. There are two types of pressure release namely: Quick and natural pressure release.

1. How to do a Ninja Foodi Quick Release

Immediately the cooking time is up, keep the venting knob on Venting Position to enable Ninja Foodi quickly release the pressure inside the pressure cooker. To release all the pressure, it normally takes some few minutes. Before you open the lid, wait until the valve drops.

2. How to do a Ninja Foodi Natural Release

Immediately the cooking time is up, you have to wait until the valve drops and the lid is opened. In order to make sure all the pressure is released before opening the lid, keep the venting knob on Venting Position. This particular pressure release technique normally takes about 10 – 25 minutes but it depends on the amount of food in your cooker. To do the 10 – 15 minutes pressure release, when the cooking time is up, wait 10 – 15 minutes before moving the Venting Knob from Sealing Position to Venting Position so as to enable the remaining pressure to be released. Do not fail to wait for the floating valve to drop before you open the lid.

Steps on How to Use Your Ninja Foodi:

This appliance is a very friendly and easy-to-use kitchen unit.

For Ninja Foodi pressure cooker:

1. Always put your foods in the inner pot of the Ninja Foodi or you put your food in the Air Fryer basket. This is basically good for meats.

2. Press the power on function.

3. Close lid in place. Do not put the one that is attached.

4. Set the top steam valve to seal position and press the pressure function.

5. Adjust the temperature to either high or low using the + or − buttons respectively.

6. Set the cooking time using the + or − buttons.

7. Press Start button.

8. The Ninja Foodi will take a little time to reach pressure and then will count the number of minutes until it reaches zero minute.

For Ninja Foodi Air Fryer:

1. Make use of the lid that is attached.

2. Place the Air Fryer cooking basket inside the Ninja Foodi inner pot.

3. Place your food inside the cooking basket.

4. Lock the attached lid and switch on the Ninja Foodi by pressing the button at the bottom.

5. Push the air crisp button.

6. Select the temperature you want to use by pressing the + and − buttons.

7. Set the cooking time by pressing the + and − buttons.

8. Select start button.

Useful Tips & Tricks for Using Your Ninja Foodi

It is pertinent to inquire to know how to properly use a new appliance you bought. Ninja Foodi come with 2 distinct lids. One is for the electric pressure cooker while the other one is for the Air Fryer lid. It is possible to use both lids in on food. Immediately the pressure cooker is done, remove the pressure cooker lid and put the Air Fryer lid. This helps to crisp your food. Every new kitchen appliance you get comes with an operational manual to guide you on the proper usage of the unit. Below are some few tips for the proper usage of your Ninja Foodi:

1. Whenever you want to spray cooking spray on the inner pot of your Ninja Foodi, do not use aerosol cooking spray.

2. Try to use the recommended amount of water or broth if you are using the pressure-cooking button. Wrong usage of water may not give you the desired result.

3. When you are not using your Ninja Foodi, unplug from any power source so as to avoid the appliance switch on by itself even when you did not press the power on button.

4. It is not advisable to use your Ninja Foodi on your stove top. This can easily damage the unit.

Ninja Foodi Troubleshooting Tips

Every electronic appliance sometimes has trouble shooting or shows a faulty message on the display. Below are some of the major trouble shooting or problems you could find on your Ninja Foodi.

1. My appliance is taking a long time to come to pressure. Why?

It is important to know how long it takes your Ninja Foodi to come to pressure. Base on a particular temperature you choose, cooking time may vary. Temperature of the cooking pot at the moment of cooking including the amount of ingredients also makes cooking time to vary. If the cooking time is taking a longer time than necessary, make sure your silicone ring is fully seated and flush against the lid, make sure the pressure lid is fully closed and set the pressure release valve to seal position.

2. Why is the cooking time counting slowly?

You have to make sure you set the time correctly. Check if you did not use hours instead of minutes. Note that the HH stands for hours while the MM stands for minutes on the display window respectively. You can increase or decrease the cooking time.

3. How do I know when the appliance is pressurizing?

When the appliance is building pressure, the rotating lights will display on the display window. When you are using steam or pressure mode, light will rotate on the display screen. It means the appliance is preheating. Immediately the preheating process finishes, the normal cooking time starts counting.

4. When I'm using the steam mode, my unit is bringing out a lot of steam.

During cooking, steam releasing on the pressure release valve is normal. It is advisable to allow the pressure release valve in the vent position for Steam, Slow Cook, and Sear or Sauté mode.

5. Why can't I take off the pressure lid?

The Ninja Foodi has to be depressurized before the pressure lid can be opened. This is one of the safety measures put by the manufacturer. In order to do a quick pressure release, set the pressure release valve to the vent position. Immediately the pressure is released completely, the lid will be ready to open.

6. Do I need to lose the pressure release valve?

The answer is yes. You have to loosen the pressure release valve. It helps to circulate pressure through some release of small amount of steam while cooking is done for the result to be excellent.

Ninja Foodi Frequently Asked Questions and Answers:

Question 1: Can I deep fry chicken with this appliance?

Answer: Yes, it is possible. You can cook a chicken in your Ninja Foodi. This is a new modern way of cooking that can tender your food and progress to crisping the food using hot air and give you a crispy result.

Question 2: Can I Take My Ninja Pot from the Refrigerator and Put directly in the appliance?

Answer: Yes, you can do it if your pot was in the refrigerator.

Question 3: Can the Pot enter under the Broiler or the Oven?

Answer: Yes. It is possible but you have to be extra careful while putting or taking the pot out from the Ninja Foodi. It is only the lid that you do not need to put under the oven or the broiler.

Question 4: Can the Baking or cooking pan enter under the oven?

Answer: Yes. It is very possible and good to put the cooking pan under the oven. You just need to be careful while inserting the pan.

Question 5: Can I use the buffet settings to cook?

Answer: NO. It is not advisable to do that because the buffet function is just to keep temperature that is above 140°F when the food has been cooked to 165°F.

Question 6: What is the meaning of One-pot Meal Cooking?

Answer: These are important family meal that could be ready within 30 minutes time. The one pot helps in a quick clean up.

Question 7: What differentiate model op301 from model op305?

Answer: Model OP305 has the Dehydrate button while model OP301 has no dehydrate button. That's the major difference.

Question 8: Can you can food with Ninja Foodi?

Answer: No, you will not be able to can food with this appliance. You can only do it if you have a pressure canner can.

Question 9: Why is the time beeper not beeping?

Answer: You can check the volume level.

Question 10: Can I put frozen pork loin in my Ninja Foodi?

Answer: Yes. It is possible to do that. Frozen foods can be cooked with this appliance.

Question 11: If the Ninja foodi displays water, what is the meaning?

Answer: It means that you need to put more water into the Ninja Foodi. If at a point of putting more water and the error still show up, contact the customer care on 877581-7375.

Question 12: Can meat and cheese vegetables be cooked with this appliance?

Answer: No. Ninja Foodi was not meant for canning of foods. So, it will not work for you.

BREAKFAST RECIPE

Bread Pudding

Preparation time: 15 minutes

Cooking time: 25 minutes

Overall time: 1 hour 3 minutes

Serves: 6 to 10 people

Recipe Ingredients:

- 1 lb. of sausage ground breakfast sausage works best
- 12 large eggs
- ¼ cup of maple syrup
- 1 cup of heavy whipping cream
- 1 teaspoon of sea salt fine grind
- 2 tablespoons of butter salted or unsalted
- 12 Hawaiian Sweet Rolls
- 1 cup of water

Optional Topping:

- 2 tablespoons of butter salted
- ¼ cup of maple syrup

Cooking Instructions:

1. Turn on your Ninja Foodi and select sear/sauté on high.

2. Add in the breakfast sausage and let it sauté and cook while you prepare the egg mixture. Use a utensil that is safe for the nonstick pan and break up the sausage.

3. don't cook the sausage all the way, but aim for about 75% done.   Crack the eggs into a blender or large bowl if you are using a hand mixer.

4. Add ¼ cup of maple syrup, 1 cup of heavy cream, and 1 tsp of fine grind sea salt. Butter the pan you are using.

5. Break up each roll into about 4 large pieces and add them to the pan or you can place them in a large bowl for easier mixing if you want.

6. Add the sausage to the bread and mix. Place into the pan, if you mixed it up in a bowl.

7. Pour the egg mixture over it and press down to make sure the egg mixture is completely covering the bread/sausage.

8. Cover the pan with foil or a silicone cover. Place it on the rack in the low position. Pour 1 cup of water into the inner pot and put the rack into the Ninja Foodi.

9. Put the pressure lid on and turn the valve to seal. Set the pressure on LOW for about 25 minutes.

10. When the time is complete, allow the Ninja Foodi to release pressure naturally for about 15 minutes.

11. Manually release the remaining pressure. Carefully remove the water from the top of the pan. Remove the cover.

12. Brush with butter and pour ¼ cup of maple syrup over the top. Turn the broil on (there's no need to preheat) and broil for about 4 to 8 minutes.

13. If the top is getting to brown, switch to the air crisp function and decrease the heat to 325°F.

14. Serve immediately and Enjoy!

Easy Homemade Biscuits

Preparation time: 10 minutes

Cooking time: 12 minutes

Overall time: 22 minutes

Serves: 7 to 10 people

Recipe Ingredients:

- 2 cups of flour all purpose, chilled
- ½ teaspoon of sea salt fine grind
- 1 tablespoon of baking powder
- 1 tablespoon of granulated white sugar
- 6 tablespoons of butter salted
- ½ cup of Greek yogurt plain, whole fat, unsweetened
- ¼ cup of water

Cooking Instructions:

1. Select the Bake function on your Ninja Foodi, set the temp for 375°F and the time for about 20 minutes.

2. Combine flour, salt, baking powder and sugar in a metal mixing bowl or a chilled glass bowl.

3. Remove the butter from the fridge and cut into ¼ inch slices into the bow with the flour.

4. Use a pastry cutter or fork to combine the flour and butter until it has a very course texture.

5. Make a well in the middle of the flour/butter mixture and pour in the Greek yogurt and water mixture.

6. Use a fork to gently combine the flour mixture and the liquid mixture. You should not have a dough yet.

7. Dump mixture onto a floured surface and press down with your fingertips until you have a 4"x 4" piece of dough.

8. Fold the top down to the bottom and turn 90° and repeat x 5, gathering all the loose flour/butter as you go.

9. Each time you press and rotate, make the square bigger, but don't go more than 8" x 8". Do not over work the dough.

10. When all the loose flour is incorporated, gently press dough down with your fingers until it is about 1" thick. Use a 2" biscuit cutter to cut out the biscuits.

11. Press straight down, don't twist, after you get as many biscuits as you can out of that dough, gently bring it back together and press it down again to 1" thick.

12. You should get at least 8 biscuits, only 8 will fit in the Ninja Foodi, place cut biscuits in a circle around the Ninja Foodi basket.

13. you should be able to get 6 or 7, depending on their size. Place one in the middle and put the basket into the inner pot.

14. Bake on 375° F for about 12 minutes. Serve and Enjoy!

Zucchini Bread

Preparation time: 10 minutes

Cooking time: 35 minutes

Overall time: 1 hour 45 minutes

Serves: 6 to 8 people

Recipe Ingredients:

- 2 large eggs
- ¾ cup of sugar
- 1 teaspoon of vanilla
- ⅓ cup of vegetable oil or canola
- 1 ½ cup of zucchini grated or 2 small zucchini
- ½ teaspoon of sea salt fine grind
- ¾ teaspoon of cloves ground
- ½ tablespoon of cinnamon ground
- 1 cup of flour
- 2 teaspoon of baking powder

Cream Cheese Icing:

- 4 oz. of cream cheese room temp
- 2 tablespoon of sugar
- ¼ cup of heavy whipping cream
- 2 tablespoons of milk

Cooking Instructions:

1. Butter and flour your loaf pan, preheat your Ninja Foodi on 275° F for about 10 minutes. Grate the zucchini using the fine side of a box grater or any grater.

2. Squeeze the liquid out of the zucchini and combine 2 eggs, ¾ cup of sugar, 1 teaspoon of vanilla, and ⅓ cup vegetable oil in a medium mixing bowl.

3. Whisk together and add in the cinnamon, cloves, salt, flour, and baking powder to the wet ingredients and stir to combine until no flour is visible flour.

4. Fold in the zucchini and pour batter into prepared loaf pan, set the loaf pan on the rack in the low position into the inner pot of the Ninja Foodi.

5. Set the Bake/Roast function to 275°F and bake for about 35 to 40 minutes. Using a thermometer, check for doneness.

6. The temp should be around 200°F. Remove and all to cool on a baking rack for about 30 to 60 minutes before applying the icing.

7. Using a hand mixer, beat the cream cheese and sugar until well combined. Add in ½ cup of heavy cream and beat for 1 minute.

8. Add in 1 tablespoon of milk and check consistency, add second tablespoon if needed. The consistency should be thick and pourable.

9. Pour over the zucchini loaf or use a pastry bag to decorate. Place bread in the refrigerator for about 60 minutes to allow the icing to set up.

10. Serve & Enjoy!

Overnight Casserole

Preparation time: 5 minutes

Cooking time: 8 hours

Overall time: 8 hours 5 minutes

Servings: 6 to 10 people

Recipe Ingredients:

- 2 Tbsp butter salted
- 1 onion ½ dice
- 1 pound of potatoes ½ dice
- 1 pound of ham cubed
- 12 Large eggs
- 1 cup heavy whipping cream
- 16 ounces cheddar cheese any kind is fine

Cooking Instructions:

1. Dice the onion into ½" dice. Turn your Ninja Foodi on High Sear/Sauté.

2. Add butter and onions, sauté for about 5 minutes. While the onions are sautéing, cut up your potatoes into ½" dice and add to the pot.

3. Crack 12 eggs into a large mixing bowl. Using an Immersion blender or whisk, blend eggs and cube the ham into bite size pieces, about 1" in size.

4. Turn off the Ninja Foodi and dump in the eggs and the heavy cream. Add the ham and the cheese and stir to combine.

5. Put the pressure lid on and turn the seal to vent. Set the Slow Cooker function to cook at low for 8 hours.

6. You can serve the casserole just as it is or top it with the remaining cup of cheddar cheese and broil for about 5 minutes or until the cheese is browned as u wish.

7. Serve immediately and Enjoy!

Banana & Caramel Steel-Cut Oats

Preparation time: 3 minutes

Cooking time: 10 minutes

Overall time: 20 minutes

Serves: 2 to 4 people

Recipe Ingredients:

- 1 cup of steel-cut oats
- 1 ½ cups of water
- ½ teaspoon of sea salt
- 2 bananas
- ¼ cup of butter
- ½ cup of brown sugar
- ¼ cup of heavy whipping cream (optional)

Cooking Instructions:

1. Combine 1 cup of steel-cut oats with 1 1/5 cups of water in the inner pot of the Ninja Foodi.

2. Add salt and sliced bananas. Stir and combine butter and brown sugar in a 6" cake pan and cover with foil.

3. Place the rack in the high position and put the cake pan on top. Put the pressure lid on and turn the valve to seal.

4. Set the pressure on LOW for about 10 minutes. When the time is complete, allow to natural release for about 7 minutes, release the remaining pressure quickly.

5. Whisk the brown sugar and butter until it is combined. Pour into the steel-cut oats and stir.

6. Serve with a tablespoon of heavy whipping cream if desired. Enjoy!

Scotch Eggs

Preparation time: 10 minutes

Cooking time: 25 minutes

Overall time: 35 minutes

Serves: 2 to 4 people

Recipe Ingredients:

- 4 Large eggs
- 8 oz. of sausage

Breading:

- ½ cup of breadcrumbs
- ½ tablespoon of maple sugar
- ⅛ teaspoon of chipotle pepper ground

Egg Mixture:

- 1 large egg
- 1 tablespoon of maple syrup
- 1 teaspoon of Cholula or your favorite hot sauce
- 1 teaspoon Dijon mustard

Dipping Sauce:

- 2 tablespoons of sour cream
- 1 teaspoon of maple sugar

Cooking Instructions:

1. Add 1 cup of cold tap water to the inner pot of the Ninja Foodi. Place the basket in the inner pot and put your eggs into the basket.

2. Put the pressure lid on and turn the valve to seal and set the pressure to high for 1 minute.

3. When the time is complete, immediately release the pressure and place the eggs into an ice bath.

4. While the eggs are cooking, mix up your breading mixture by combining bread crumbs and make sugar in a round bowl that is at least 3" deep.

5. Combine 1 egg with maple syrup, mustard and hot sauce and mix to combine. Dump the water from the inner pot of the Ninja Foodi.

6. Preheat on broil for a full 10 minutes with the basket inside the Ninja Foodi. If you aren't done with the wrapping and breading of your eggs in 10 minutes.

7. Turn the broil on for another 10 minutes and when you are done preparing your eggs, you can switch from broil to Air Crisp.

8. Press 2 ounces of sausage into an oval or round shape that is about ⅛-¼" thick. Place the peeled egg in the center and gently wrap the sausage around the egg.

9. Dip the sausage encased egg into the egg mixture and coat. Dip into the breading mixture and coat completely.

10. Repeat this step for a second coating. When the Ninja Foodi has preheated for 10 minutes on broil, spritz the basket with oil.

11. Place the scotch eggs in the basket and spritz them with oil. Select the Air Crisp function on 375°F for about 7 minutes.

12. You don't have to flip, if you aren't serving the Scotch Eggs right away, place them on a cooling rack and not a flat plate to avoid steaming the underside.

13. Combine sour cream with maple sugar and serve as a drizzle over the eggs or as a dipping sauce.

14. Slice the Scotch eggs in half with a sharp knife and serve. Enjoy!

Quick & Easy Orange Marmalade

Preparation time: 5 minutes

Cooking time: 40 minutes

Overall time: 1 hour 15 minutes

Serves: 6 to 8 people

Recipe Ingredients:

- 1 pound of mandarin oranges about 5-6 small oranges
- 2 cups of water
- 3 cups of sugar divided in recipe

Cooking Instructions:

1. Cut off the stem of the mandarins and slice the mandarins in half. Slice each half into slices about ¼" thick.

2. Throw them in the inner pot of the Ninja Foodi and add 2 cups of water and 2½ cups of white sugar. Stir.

3. Put the pressure lid on the Ninja Foodi and turn the valve to seal. Select high pressure for about 10 minutes.

4. When the time is complete, allow the pot to naturally release its pressure, this takes about 25 minutes.

5. Open the lid and turn on the sear/sauté on high and bring the mixture to a boil and add in remaining ½ cup of sugar.

6. Bring back up to a boil and boil until the mixture reaches about 221°F. This is important in order for your marmalade to set up.

7. Using a thermometer check for doneness, once the orange marmalade has reached at least 221°F, turn off the heat and stir.

8. Allow to cool and then ladle into jars and let them sit at room temperature for 1 to 2 hours, then refrigerate at least 4 hours to set up.

9. Serve & Enjoy

Huevos Rancheros

Preparation time: 10 minutes

Cooking time: 13 minutes

Overall time: 23 minutes

Serves: 2 to 4 people

Recipe Ingredients:

- 2 tbsp. of canola oil, divided
- 1 small onion, peeled, diced
- 3 cloves of garlic, peeled, roughly chopped
- 1 can (15.5 oz.) of black beans, rinsed, drained
- 3 tsp. of kosher salt, divided
- ½ tsp. of ground cumin
- ¼ cup of water
- 6 large eggs, beaten
- ½ cup of queso fresco, crumbled, divided
- 4 corn tostadas (6 inches each)
- 1 cup of fresh or chunky salsa
- ¼ cup of fresh cilantro, finely chopped
- 1 avocado, peeled, pit removed, thinly sliced

Cooking Instructions:

1. Select sear/sauté and set to md:hi. select start/stop to begin. allow to preheat for about 5 minutes.

2. Add 1 tablespoon of oil and onion to pot and sauté for about 3 minutes. add garlic and sauté for 1 minute. Add beans, 1 teaspoon salt, cumin, and water to pot.

3. Stir to incorporate and assemble pressure lid, make sure the pressure release valve is in seal position. Select pressure and set to high and set time to 3 minutes.

4. Select start/stop to begin. while beans are cooking, combine ¼ cup of queso fresco and remaining salt with the beaten eggs.

5. When the pressure cooking is complete, quick release the pressure by moving the pressure release valve to the vent position.

6. Carefully remove lid when unit has finished releasing pressure. Remove beans from the pot and transfer to a small mixing bowl, mashing lightly with a fork.

7. Select sear/sauté and set to md:hi. select start/stop to begin. add remaining oil, then pour in the egg mixture.

8. Cook eggs, stirring constantly, for about 3 minutes, or until scrambled. remove eggs from pot.

9. Spread mashed bean mixture onto each tostada, then add eggs, salsa, and avocado. garnish with remaining queso fresco and cilantro.

10. Serve immediately and Enjoy!

Corned Beef Hash

Preparation time: 15 minutes

Cooking time: 35 minutes

Overall time: 50 minutes

Serves: 4 to 6 people

Recipe Ingredients:

- ½ lb. of cooked corned beef, diced
- 2 tbsp. of vegetable oil
- 1 white onion, peeled, finely chopped
- 1 bell pepper, finely chopped
- 2 medium baking potatoes, peeled, diced
- ½ tsp. of ground black pepper
- 3 tsp. of kosher salt, divided
- 6 large eggs
- Hot sauce, for serving

Cooking Instructions:

1. Select sear/sauté and set to high, select start/stop to begin. Allow to preheat for 5 minutes.

2. Add corned beef to pot and sauté for about 5 minutes, or until fat has rendered. Add oil, onion, pepper, and potatoes to pot.

3. Season with pepper and 2 teaspoons salt. sauté for about 5 to 10 minutes, until onions are translucent and peppers have softened.

4. Then let the onions and peppers cook for another 5 minutes, without stirring, so that a crust forms on the bottom.

5. When the time is complete, stir mixture and let cook for another 5 minutes, without stirring.

6. Crack eggs onto the surface on the hash and season with remaining salt. close the crisping lid.

7. Select broil and set time to 10 minutes. check eggs frequently, cooking until desired doneness.

8. When cooking is complete, serve eggs and hash immediately with hot sauce.

Frittata

Preparation time: 15 minutes

Cooking time: 25 minutes

Overall time: 40 minutes

Serves: 4 to 6 people

Recipe Ingredients:

- 3 tbsp. of extra virgin olive oil
- 2 medium leeks, white and pale green parts only, thinly sliced, rinsed thoroughly
- 1 package (8 oz.) of cremini mushrooms, thinly sliced
- 12 large eggs
- ½ cup of crème fraiche
- 2 tbsp. of fresh parsley, minced
- 1 cup of shredded Swiss-Gruyère cheese, divided
- ¼ tsp. of kosher salt
- ¼ tsp. of freshly ground black pepper
- 1 cup of water

Cooking Instructions:

1. Select sear/sauté and set to md:hi. Press the start/stop button to begin. add oil and allow to preheat for about 5 minutes.

2. When the 5 minutes is up, add leeks and cook until softened, about 5 minutes. then add mushrooms and cook, stirring often, until liquid has evaporated.

3. While the mushrooms are cooking, whisk together the eggs, crème fraiche, and parsley in a large bowl and stir in ¾ cup of cheese, salt, and pepper.

4. Once the liquid has evaporated, remove mushrooms and leeks from the pot and stir into the egg mixture.

5. Add water to the pot and place the ninja pan (or 8-inch baking pan) on the reversible rack, making sure rack is in the lower position.

6. Place rack with pan in pot and close the crisping lid. Preheat the unit by selecting broil and setting time to 5 minutes.

7. Press the start/stop button to begin. when unit is preheated, open the crisping lid and generously spray the pan with cooking spray.

8. Pour egg mixture into the pan, assemble the pressure lid, making sure the pressure release valve is in the seal position.

9. Select pressure and set to high, set the time to 10 minutes. Press the start/stop button to begin.

10. when pressure cooking is complete, allow the pressure to release naturally for 10 minutes.

11. After the 10 minutes of natural pressure release, quick release the remaining pressure by moving the pressure release valve to the vent position.

12. carefully remove lid when unit has finished releasing pressure. Pat the surface of the frittata with a paper towel to remove excess moisture.

13. Sprinkle another ¼ cup of cheese on top. close the crisping lid, select broil, and set time to 7 minutes. press the start/stop button to begin.

14. When cooking is complete, frittata is ready to serve.

Soup & Stew Recipes

Gazpacho

Preparation time: 20 minutes

Cooking time: 3 hours

Overall time: 3 hr. 20 minutes

Serves: 5 to 8 people

Recipe Ingredients

- ½ small red onion, peeled, cut in quarters
- ½ English cucumber, cut in 2-inch pieces
- ½ green bell pepper, cut in quarters
- ½ red bell pepper, cut in quarters
- lb. of fresh vine-ripe tomatoes, cut in quarters
- ½ jalapeño, seeds removed, cut in quarters
- tbsp. of red wine vinegar
- Juice of 1 lime
- tbsp. of olive oil
- 2 tsp. of salt
- cups of tomato juice

Cooking Instructions:

1. Add all ingredients, except tomato juice, into the 64-ounce Precision Processor in the order listed. Select Chop function button on your Ninja.

2. Add tomato juice and select Cook Low function button on your Ninja for 5 seconds, or until desired consistency is reached.

3. Now serve and enjoy hot.

Roasted Butternut Squash & Apple Soup

Preparation time: 10 minutes

Cooking time: 50 minutes

Overall time: 60 minutes

Serves: 2 to 4 people

Recipe Ingredients

- 2 cups of butternut squash, peeled, cut in 1-inch pieces
- 1 green apple, cut in quarters, sliced
- 2 cloves of garlic, peeled
- 2 tablespoons of olive oil
- 1 tsp. of salt, divided
- ¼ tsp. of paprika
- 2 cups of chicken stock
- Pinch ground black pepper

Cooking Instructions

1. Now preheat Ninja oven to 400°F. Place butternut squash, apple, and garlic onto baking sheet.

2. Drizzle with olive oil and ½ teaspoon salt. Toss to evenly coat. Roast for 40 minutes.

3. Sprinkle with paprika, then place back in oven and roast for another 5 minutes. Carefully remove mixture from oven and let cool for about 15 to 20 minutes.

4. Place the High-Speed Blade into the Jar, then add cooled squash mixture, chicken stock, 1/2 teaspoon salt, and pepper.

5. Pulse 3 times, then run continuously for 60 seconds or until desired consistency is achieved.

6. Transfer soup to medium pot over medium-high heat and cook for 10 minutes, or until heated through.

Zucchini and Summer Squash Soup

Preparation time: 5 minutes

Cooking time: 10 minutes

Total time: 15 minutes

Serves: 2 to 3 people

Recipe Ingredients

- 1 medium white onion, peeled and chopped
- 3 garlic cloves, peeled and minced
- 2 tablespoons of olive oil
- 3 summer squash, sliced
- 3 zucchinis, sliced
- 3 cups of vegetable broth

Cooking Instructions

1. Set Ninja to medium high heat pressure, place the onion, garlic and olive oil into a sauce pot and heat for 5 to 8 minutes or until brown.

2. Add the squash, zucchini and broth and bring to a boil. Once vegetables are tender,

3. Gently remove from heat and allow the mixture to cool. Finally, transfer the mixture to the 40 oz. Blender and blend until it's smooth.

4. Refrigerate and serve chilled.

Kale and Leek Soup

Preparation time: 5 minutes

Cooking time: 25 minutes

Total time: 30 minutes

Serves: 3 to 4 people

Recipe Ingredients

- 2 teaspoons of olive oil
- leek, cleaned and sliced
- 4 cups of kale, chopped and stems removed
- cups of vegetable broth
- Salt and pepper to taste

Cooking Instructions:

1. Heat olive oil in a sauté pan over Ninja medium high heat pressure mode. Add leek and kale and cook until softened and wilted.

2. Add the vegetable broth and cook over medium heat for 20 to 25 minutes or so and then remove from heat.

3. Once cooled, transfer the soup into the 40 oz. Blender and blend until smooth. Microwave or return to pot and heat through.

4. Serve and enjoy.

Strawberry Orange Summer Soup

Preparation time: 5 minutes

Cooking time: 5 minutes

Gross minutes: 10 minutes

Serves 4 to 6 people

Recipe Ingredients:

- 4 cups of strawberries, hulled
- 1 cup of strawberry yogurt
- 1 cup of orange juice
- 2 tablespoons of fresh mint, chopped
- 2 teaspoons of grated orange zest
- 1 teaspoon of agave

Cooking Instructions:

1. Place ingredients into the 72 oz. Ninja Pitcher blend and blend until its smooth.

2. Serve immediately or chill before serving.

Sausage & Cabbage Soup

Preparation time: 5 minutes

Cooking time: 10 minutes

Overall time: 15 minutes

Serves: 4 to 6 people

Recipe Ingredients:

- 2 cups of potatoes, peeled and cubed
- 4 cups of shredded cabbage
- 1 carrot shredded, (we bought the pre-shredded and used about ½ the package of 1 large onion)
- 1¼ pounds of sausage
- 4 cups of chicken broth or you can water
- Salt and pepper to taste

Cooking Directions:

1. Place all dry ingredients in your Ninja and pour liquid on top.

2. Cover and set Ninja to cook on Slow Cook at Low pressure function mode for 8 to 10 hours, or High-pressure function mode for 5 hours.

3. Serve immediately and enjoy!

Shipwreck

Preparation time: 5 minutes

Cooking time: 10 minutes

Gross time: 15 minutes

Serves: 2 to 4 people

Recipe Ingredients:

- 1 pound of ground beef
- 1 onion, chopped
- 1 bell pepper or jalapeño - optional
- 2 cans of Campbell's tomato soup. (We use healthy choice)
- 1 soup can, filled with water
- salt and pepper to taste
- 1 can of diced potatoes, drained
- 1 can of kidney beans - (drained)

Cooking Instructions:

1. Turn the Ninja to Stove Top High. Add the beef and onion to brown; also add the bell peppers or jalapeño, if desired. Drain.

2. Add the remaining ingredients and stir gently until they are well combined.

3. Turn the Ninja to Stove to cook at High pressure for 20 minutes. If you would rather have a slow cook meal; turn the Ninja to cook at Slow Low pressure for 4 hours.

4. You can also use the Ninja Oven setting of 350°F for 30 minutes. If choosing the Oven setting, we suggest stirring a few times.

5. Serve and enjoy.

Spicy Beef & Potato Soup

Preparation time: 10 minutes

Cooking time: 50 minutes

Overall time: 60 minutes

Serves: 2 to 4 people

Recipe Ingredients:

- 1 Pounds of hamburger
- 2 teaspoons of salt
- 1 teaspoon of black pepper
- 1 chopped onion
- 4 cups of diced potatoes
- 24 ounces of tomato sauce
- 4 cups of water
- ½ to 1 tablespoon Tabasco – or to taste

Cooking Instructions:

1. Turn your Ninja setting to Stove mode, select pressure function to cook at high pressure to brown the beef.

2. Add the salt, pepper, onions, potatoes, tomato sauce, water and Tabasco sauce.

3. Bring it to a boil. Turn your Ninja to Stove Top Low and cook for an hour, or until the potatoes are fork tender.

4. Serve and enjoy.

Turkey Vegetable Soup

Preparation time: 8 minutes

Cooking time: 8 hours

Overall time: 8 hr. 8 minutes

Serves: 2 to 5 people

Recipe Ingredients

- ½ stick of butter or margarine
- 1 large onion, chopped
- Dark meat turkey, (1-quart Zip-Lock bag from thanksgiving)
- 16 ounces mixed vegetables
- 15 ounces can of corn
- 2 cans of sliced carrots, (drained of liquid)
- 32 ounces of box of chicken broth
- 2 cans of water from the carrots

Cooking Ingredients:

1. Turn the Ninja to Stove Top High-pressure mode. Add butter or margarine. Then select Sauté on Ninja and Sauté onion.

2. While the onions are sautéing, chop up the turkey. Add turkey, mixed vegetables, corn, sliced carrots, chicken broth and water to the Ninja pot.

3. Stir continuously until well combined. Turn the Ninja to Slow Cook Low for 8 hours.

4. Soup is ready; serve and enjoy with dinner rolls.

Tuscan White Bean Stew

Preparation time: 5 minutes

Cooking time: 6 hours

Overall time: 6 hr. 5 minutes

Serves: 8 to 10 people

Recipe Ingredients:

- 3 tablespoons. Olive Oil
- 1 medium onion, diced
- 2 Ribs of celery, cut into ½ inch pieces
- 2 Carrots, cut into 1-inch pieces
- 8 cloves of garlic, smashed
- 1 Pound of dried cannellini beans
- 4 cups of chicken broth
- 4 cups of water
- 2 bay leaves
- 2 tsp. of salt
- ½ tsp. of pepper
- Spinach or kale or both
- 1 can of diced tomatoes
- 1 Pound of Kielbasa (purchase pre-cooked and pre-cut into "½" slices).

Cooking Instructions:

1. Turn the Ninja to Stove mode at Medium/High pressure function. Select Sauté on Ninja and Sauté onion, carrots and celery in olive oil until soft.

2. Add the garlic and sauté for a minute more. Add the beans, broth, water, salt and pepper. Stir gently until well combined.

3. Turn the Ninja to Slow Cook Low for 6 hours. After the cook time, add the kielbasa, spinach, kale, (or both), and tomatoes and cook until kale is tender.

4. Remove bay leaves before serving.

Unstuffed Pepper Stew

Preparation time: 5 minutes

Cooking time: 30 minutes

Overall time: 35 minutes

Serves: 4 to 6 people

Recipe Ingredients:

- 2 lbs. of sweet ground Italian sausage
- 1 large sweet onion, cut into slivers
- 2 bell peppers, cut into slivers
- 2 cups of rice
- 2 cups of water
- 24 oz. jar of spaghetti sauce
- 14.5 oz. can of stewed tomatoes
- Cheddar cheese
- Mozzarella cheese
- Italian seasoning
- Garlic powder
- Pepper
- Chives
- Sliced black olives

Cooking Instructions:

1. Turn the Ninja to Stove mode of High pressure. Cook the sausage, onions, and peppers until sausage is cooked through and peppers and onions softened.

2. Add the rice, water, stewed tomatoes and spices. Cover until rice is well cooked.

3. Stir occasionally. Add spaghetti sauce. Stir. Cover for about 5 minutes. Scoop into bowls and sprinkle cheeses, a few black olives and chives.

4. Serve immediately and enjoy your meal. Delicious!

Vegetable Beef Soup

Preparation time: 10 minutes

Cooking time: 6 hours

Overall time: 6 hr. 10 minutes

Serve: 2 to 4 people

Recipe Ingredients:

- 1 beef soup bone
- 4 stalks of celery, cut up
- ½ large onion, chopped
- 32 ounces of box of beef broth
- 15 ounces can of diced tomatoes
- 16 ounces of bag mixed vegetables
- 2 small potatoes, peeled and chopped
- Garlic, salt & pepper (to taste)
- 2 bay leaves
- 1-quart of water
- Spinach (optional)

Cooking Instructions:

1. Add all of the ingredients to the Ninja pot, (except spinach) and turn Ninja to cook at slow cook Low pressure function for 4 to 6 hours.

2. Allow unit to switch to Auto Warm or switch to Buffet setting to hold. Add the spinach at the end if desired.

3. Remove bay leaves before serving.

Nicoise Chicken Stew

Preparation time: 10 minutes

Cooking time: 1 hour 30 minutes

Gross time: 1 hour 40 minutes

Serves: 1 to 3 people

Recipe Ingredients:

- 2 Pounds of chicken pieces
- 10 garlic cloves, peeled
- 25 to 30 nicoise olives
- 28 ounces diced tomatoes
- 2 cups of chicken stock
- 2 tablespoons of fresh rosemary, minced
- 2 tablespoons of fresh thyme, minced
- 2 tablespoons of fresh basil, minced
- 2 tablespoons of fresh parsley, minced
- Cooking fat
- Sea salt and freshly ground black pepper

Cooking Instructions:

1. Turn your Ninja to Stove Top High and select sauté function on the Ninja to sauté your garlic. Remove after sauté.

2. Add your seasoned chicken and brown evenly on all sides. Add the garlic, tomatoes, olives, chicken stock, rosemary, thyme, basil and parsley.

3. Cover and turn your Ninja to 325°F for 1 hours 30 minutes. (We did not use the multipurpose pan. It's directly in the Ninja pot.)

4. But if you have time, you can add everything and set Ninja to cook on slow cook pressure for 2 to 4 hours.

5. Test the chicken with a digital thermometer and add more time if necessary.

6. Serve and enjoy.

Chicken Stew

Preparation time: 5 minutes

Cooking time: 6 hours

Overall time: 6 hours 5 minutes

Serves: 2 to 4 people

Recipe Ingredients:

- 4 chicken breasts cut in cubes
- 3 to 4 potatoes, diced
- 2 to 3 stalks celery, diced
- 3 to 4 carrots, diced
- 2 cans (10 ounces, each) of cream of chicken soup
- 1 chicken of bouillon cube
- 2 tsp. of garlic salt
- 1 tsp. pepper
- 16-ounce bag frozen mixed vegetables

Cooking Instructions:

1. Add cubed chicken and fresh vegetables to your Ninja. Pour soup overall and add seasonings

2. Turn Ninja to Slow Cook High and cook for 4 to 5 hours. Add the frozen vegetables and continue cooking for 1 more hour

3. Let the unit go to Auto Warm or turn it to Buffet setting to hold until ready to eat.

4. Serve immediately and enjoy!

Baked Beef Stew

Preparation time: 5 minutes

Cooking time: 45 minutes

Overall time: 50 Minutes

Serves: 3 to 5 people

Recipe Ingredients:

- 2 packages stew meat cut into small pieces
- 4 large potatoes diced
- ½ package baby carrots (or small bag)
- 1 onion diced
- 1 can of tomato soup
- 1 can of water
- 2 tablespoon of tapioca (minute)
- 2 Tablespoon of Worcestershire Sauce
- Salt and pepper

Cooking Instructions:

1. Use all the above ingredients and layer in the Ninja.

2. Set Ninja to oven mode of 300°F and bake for about 45 minutes. After 45 minutes.

3. Serve immediately and enjoy!

POULTRY RECIPE

Chicken Legs

Preparation time: 5 minutes

Cooking time: 25 minutes

Overall time: 30 minutes

Serves: 2 to 4 people

Recipe Ingredients:

- 10 medium chicken legs
- ½ cup of barbecue sauce give or take
- 1 cup of water

Cooking Instructions:

1. Put chicken legs in a bowl with ¼ cup barbeque sauce and mix so they're coated, using hands works well for this.

2. Pour cup of water into your Foodi and lower down air fryer basket that came with your pot with holes in bottom and handles on the sides.

3. Put coated chicken legs into basket. Close pressure cooker lid (one not attached), and steam valve.

4. Press pressure cook button, will automatically set to high, and set for about 12 minutes.

5. When done do a quick release for the steam inside the pot. Use tongs to carefully remove the legs on to a plate.

6. You can drain the water out now if you wish. Spray the inside of your basket with nonstick cooking spray.

7. Lay one layer of legs back into the basket, do not overlap them at this time. Use a brush to add the remaining ¼ cup of barbeque sauce on to the drumsticks now.

8. Close air crisp lid and set to 400°F for about 10 minutes. Check, if you want them crispier, set for a few more minutes.

9. Remove this batch, put in the next and enjoy when they're all done.

Crack Chicken

Preparation time: 10 minutes

Cooking time: 15 minutes

Overall time: 25 minutes

Serves: 2 to 4 people

Recipe Ingredients:

- 2 pounds of chicken breasts boneless skinless breasts cut in half
- 1 block cream cheese room temperature
- ½ cup of chicken broth
- ½ onion diced
- 1 packet of ranch dressing mix
- 4 slices of bacon cooked, broken into bits
- 2 teaspoons of cornstarch optional
- 2 cup of cheese we use Mexican blend, cheddar is great too

Cooking Instructions:

1. Set your pot to sauté and add fresh diced bacon with 1 tablespoon of olive oil and your diced onions. Cook until bacon is cooked but not super crispy.

2. if you previously cooked your bacon turn off your pot. Add chicken evenly across bottom of pot.

3. Then cut chunks of room temp and cream cheese into smaller chunks and add on top of chicken.

4. Add onions, followed by sprinkling in your packet of dry ranch dressing mix over the top. Pour your chicken broth on top of everything evenly.

5. Close your pressure cooker lid and steam valve, set to 15 minutes for halved chicken breasts, or about 12 minutes if you're using thinner chicken tenders.

6. Do a quick release when the cook time is up, take some of the hot broth out of the pot and add it to your bowl with cornstarch in it.

7. Whisk that together so it is smooth. Shred your chicken with 2 forks inside the pot.

8. Stir contents so cream cheese becomes smooth and chicken is coated with mixture.

9. for a thicker mix turn Foodi to sauté and once it bubbles add your smooth cornstarch mix and stir so it thickens.

10. Then turn pot off and stir in cooked bacon and shredded cheese so it melts. Top with green onions or chives.

11. Serve on slider or hamburger buns.

Roast Chicken

Preparation time: 10 minutes

Cooking time: 30 minutes

Overall time: 40 minutes

Serves: 2 to 4 people

Recipe Ingredients:

- 1 whole chicken, (3.5 - 4 pounds)
- 1 cup of water
- 2 drops of liquid smoke
- As desired salt and pepper
- 2 tablespoons of butter
- 1 teaspoon of paprika
- 1 teaspoon of garlic powder
- ½ teaspoon of onion powder
- 1 teaspoon of seasoned salt
- As desired, pepper
- ¼ cup of flour
- 2 cup of chicken stock

For the Basting Butter:

- 2 tablespoons of butter
- Dash of garlic powder
- As desired, seasoning salt and pepper

Cooking Instructions:

1. Wash and pat dry the chicken and season inside and out with seasoned salt, pepper, paprika, garlic and onion powders.

2. Mix the water and the liquid smoke together and pour into the main pot of the Foodi and place the chicken in the basket, inside the main pot of the Foodi.

3. Cook on high pressure for about 15 minutes. When the time is complete, do a quick release, remove the chicken and the basket.

4. Discard the water that was in the bottom of the Foodi bowl. Replace the chicken and the basket inside the Foodi liner and place the liner back into the unit.

5. In a small bowl, melt the butter and make up the basting butter recipe above. Air crisp at 400°F for about 15 minutes.

6. Lift the lid occasionally, basting the chicken with your basting butter to crisp/brown it to your desired color.

7. Remove the chicken and the basket, and cover with tin foil to continue cooking to reach a 165°F temperature reading.

8. In the Foodi bowl, add the butter and flour to the drippings and press sauté. Mix everything together and slowly, add the stock in small increments as it thickens.

9. When all the liquid is added and thickened, you are ready to serve!   Enjoy!

Mexican Shredded Chicken

Preparation time: 5 minutes

Cooking time: 45 minutes

Overall time: 50 minutes

Serves: 4 to 6 people

Recipe Ingredients:

- 14.5 oz. of fire roasted tomatoes
- 1 cup of chicken stock
- ½ onion
- 1 jalapeno pepper
- 2 teaspoons of sea salt fine grind
- 2 teaspoons of cumin
- 1 teaspoon of garlic powder
- 1 teaspoon of onion powder
- 1 bunch of cilantro stems only for this recipe
- 1½ pounds of chicken breasts (boneless, skinless) frozen or thawed

Cooking Instructions:

1. Add the fire roasted tomatoes, chicken stock, diced onion, sliced jalapeno pepper, and spices to the inner pot of the Ninja Foodi.

2. Stir to combine the spices. Cut the stems off of 1 bunch of cilantro and chop into about ½" size and add to the pot.

3. Reserve the cilantro leaves for garnish in the dish you make with the shredded chicken.

4. Nestle the chicken breasts into the pot and try to get them as submerged as possible.

5. Put the pressure lid on and turn the valve to seal. Set the pressure on high for about 25 minutes.

6. When the time is up, allow the pot to natural release the pressure for about 10 minutes and then manually release the remaining pressure.

7. Use a Mix 'N Chop to shred the chicken right in the pot. Use in your favorite Mexican dish and enjoy!

Turkey Breast

Preparation time: 10 minutes

Cooking time: 8 minutes

Overall time: 45 minutes

Serves: 4 to 6 people

Recipe Ingredients:

- 6 lb. of turkey breast Bone-in
- 2 teaspoons of sea salt fine grind
- 1 teaspoon of pepper
- 1 carrot
- ½ onion
- 2 stalks of celery
- 3 cloves of garlic
- 3 sprigs of rosemary
- 4 sprigs of thyme
- 2 orange wedges

Compound Butter:

- 4 tablespoons of butter salted
- 2 cloves of minced garlic about 1 tsp
- 1 teaspoon of sea salt fine grind
- ½ teaspoon of black pepper
- ½ teaspoon of thyme leaves dried
- ½ teaspoon of rosemary dried and crushed
- ½ teaspoon of onion powder

Cooking Instructions:

1. Thaw and rinse your turkey, pat dry with paper towels. Mix the salt and pepper together in a small bowl.

2. Sprinkle the seasoning over the skin and pat it in. Also sprinkle some of the seasoning into the turkey cavity.

3. Place ½ carrot, 1 stalk of celery, ½ onion, 2 garlic cloves, 3 sprigs of rosemary, 4 stems of thyme, and 2 orange wedges into the cavity.

4. Depending on the size of your turkey breast, you may have to reduce the quantity of these ingredient so they fit inside the cavity.

5. Determine what you will sit your turkey breast on depending on size. While you can sit it directly in the inner pot.

6. Add the remaining ½ carrot, celery stalk and ends, and clove of garlic to the inner pot and pour in one cup of chicken bone broth.

7. Put the pressure lid on and turn the valve to seal. Set the pressure time to 8 minutes for a 6 pound of turkey.

8. When the time is completed, allow the pressure to be released naturally for about 15 minutes. While the pressure is being released, mix up your compound butter.

9. Combine room temperature butter, minced garlic, and seasonings until the seasonings are incorporated into the butter.

10. Remove the turkey from the Ninja Foodi and place on paper towels to absorb the excess moisture.

11. Pat the skin dry with a clean towel or a paper towel and allow to cool for a few minutes.

12. Dump the stock from the inner pot into a mixing bowl. Preheat the Ninja Foodi on Air Crisp at 400°F for about 10 minutes.

13. Lift up the skin a little bit and place some of the compound butter under the skin and move it around under the skin.

14. Repeat this until you use about ½ of the compound butter. Then rub the remaining butter on top of the turkey skin.

15. Place the turkey back into the inner pot using the rack, sling, or you can even sit it right on the bottom. Make this decision based on the size of your turkey breast.

16. Ensure you have few inches between the heating element and the highest part of the turkey breast.

17. Air Crisp on 400°F for about 10 to 14 minutes, make sure to check on it every 2 minutes after the first 6 minutes to make sure it doesn't start to burn.

18. Remove and allow to rest for 10 minutes.   Carve & Enjoy!

Whole Turkey

Preparation time: 10 minutes

Cooking time: 15 minutes

Overall time: 58 minutes

Serves: 6 to 8 people

Recipe Ingredients:

Seasoning Blend for Turkey Rub:

- 4 tablespoons of paprika
- 4 teaspoon of sea salt
- 2 teaspoons of poultry seasoning
- 2 teaspoons of red pepper flakes
- 2 teaspoons of garlic powder
- 2 teaspoons of black pepper course
- 1 teaspoons of rosemary dried

For the Turkey:

- 8 pounds of turkey
- 2 stalks of celery
- 4 cloves of garlic
- ½ onion
- 1 orange
- 3 sprigs of rosemary

Cooking Instructions:

1. Pat the turkey dry after rinsing and stuff the cavity with the celery, onion, peeled garlic cloves, orange slices, and rosemary.

2. Rub the seasoning blend all over the turkey. You won't be needing all of it, but reserve the rest for later.

3. Place the turkey on a silicone sling or you make one out of foil. Add ½ cup of water into the inner pot. Lower the sling with the turkey into the inner pot.

4. Put the pressure lid on and turn the valve to seal. Select high pressure and set the time to 15 minutes.

5. Let the turkey natural release for about 15 minutes and then release the remaining pressure manually.

6. Check the temperature, it should read at least 160°F. If the temperature has not reached 160° F, you can bring it up to the correct temperature by roasting.

7. The temperature will rise an additional 5 to 10°F during the crisping or while it rests.

8. You can crisp the skin using the Roast or Broil function on the Ninja Foodi If your turkey is small enough.

9. You can crisp the skin in the oven. Carve and serve the turkey and Enjoy!

Garlic Parmesan Chicken Wings

Preparation time: 10 minutes

Cooking time: 21 minutes

Overall time: 31 minutes

Serves: 5 to 7 people

Recipe Ingredients:

- 12 Chicken wings
- 1 tablespoon of olive oil
- 1 cup of chicken broth
- 1/3 cup of butter
- 1 teaspoon of garlic, minced
- 1 teaspoon of garlic powder
- 1/3 cup of parmesan cheese, grated
- ¼ teaspoon of Italian seasoning, dried
- ¼ teaspoon of lemon juice

Cooking Instructions:

1. Lay your washed chicken wings out on a board.

2. Pat dry and season with garlic powder, salt and pepper. Place the wings into a zip lock bag and add the olive oil.

3. Seal the bag and squish the wings around to distribute the seasoning well. Marinate for about 30 minutes or more.

4. Pour the chicken broth in the bottom of the Ninja Foodi bowl insert and place the wings in the broth. Cover with the pressure-cooking lid.

5. Place the toggle switch into the seal position. Pressure cook for about 7 minutes, do a quick pressure release. While the wings are cooking, make the basting sauce.

6. Melt the butter and then add the salt and pepper, Italian seasoning, lemon juice, minced garlic, and parmesan cheese.

7. Taste for your seasoning preference, make any adjustments if needed. Remove the wings and place the crisping rack in the insert bowl.

8. Place the wings on the top rack and begin to air fry. Use the air fry function at 400°F for about 15 minutes.

9. Air crisped them for approximately 12 minutes. As they air crisp, you will want to keep basting the wings with your garlic parmesan sauce.

10. Put as much or as little on as you like until you've reached your desired crispiness.

11. Serve immediately and Enjoy!

Chicken Wings

Preparation time: 5 minutes

Cooking time: 21 minutes

Overall time: 26 minutes

Serves: 2 to 4 people

Recipe Ingredients:

- 24 chicken wings defrosted or fresh, depending on size
- ¾ cup of brown sugar
- 1.5 tablespoons of salt
- 1 tablespoon of garlic salt
- 1 teaspoon of pepper
- 2 tablespoons of garlic powder
- 1 tablespoon of chili powder
- ¾ tablespoon of paprika
- ¾ tablespoon of cayenne pepper for medium heat, less if you want them mild
- Olive oil spray

Cooking Instructions:

1. Close air crisp lid and preheat Foodi to 400°F.

2. Pat wings dry with paper towels. In batches of 6-8 pieces, spray batch with olive oil spray and rub on all sides.

3. In a bowl mix all dry rub ingredients and pour half inside a freezer bag, add olive oil coated wings into bag and shake so they're well coated.

4. Place wings inside air fryer basket without overlapping them. Air fry for about 8 minutes, then flip to other side.

5. Continue to cook at 400°F for another 8 minutes or until they're as crispy as you'd like.

6. To make even crispier, lightly spray top again with olive oil spray and continue cooking a few more minutes.

7. Serve immediately and Enjoy!

Buffalo Chicken Wings

Preparation time: 10 minutes

Cooking time: 20 minutes

Overall time: 30 minutes

Serves: 4 to 6 people

Recipe Ingredients:

- ½ cup of water
- 2 lb. of frozen chicken wings, drums and flats separated
- 2 tbsp. of canola oil
- 2 tbsp. of buffalo sauce
- 2 tsp. of kosher salt

Cooking Instructions:

1. Pour water into pot and place wings into the cook & crisp basket and place basket in pot.

2. Assemble the pressure lid, making sure the pressure release valve is in the seal position.

3. Select pressure and set high. set time to 5 minutes. Press the start/stop button to begin.

4. When pressure cooking is complete, quick release the pressure by turning the pressure release valve to the vent position.

5. Carefully remove lid when unit has finished releasing pressure. pat wings dry with paper towels and toss with 2 tablespoons of oil in the basket.

6. Close crisping lid, select air crisp and set temperature to 390°F, and set time to 15 minutes. Press the start/stop button to begin.

7. After 7 minutes, open lid, then lift basket and shake wings or toss them with silicone-tipped tongs. lower basket back into pot and close lid to resume cooking.

8. While the wings are cooking, stir together buffalo sauce and salt in a large mixing bowl.

9. When cooking is complete, transfer wings to the bowl with buffalo sauce and toss to coat. Serve immediately and Enjoy!

Herb-Roasted Chicken

Preparation time: 10 minutes

Cooking time: 41 minutes

Overall time: 51 minutes

Serves: 2 to 4 people

Recipe Ingredients:

- (5 pounds) 1 whole uncooked chicken
- (¼) cup of lemon juice) Juice of 2 lemons
- ¼ cup of hot water
- 1/4 cup of honey
- 3 tbsp. of kosher salt, divided
- 1 tbsp. of whole black peppercorns
- 5 sprigs of fresh thyme
- 5 cloves of garlic, peeled, smashed
- 1 tbsp. of canola oil
- 2 tsp. of ground black pepper

Cooking Instructions:

1. Remove packet of giblets, if it is included in cavity of the chicken. rinse chicken and tie legs together with cooking twine.

2. mix together lemon juice, hot water, honey, and 2 tablespoons salt in a small bowl and pour mixture into the pot.

3. Place whole peppercorns, thyme, and garlic in the pot, place chicken into the cook & crisp basket and place basket in pot.

4. Assemble pressure lid, making sure the pressure release valve is in the seal position. select pressure and set to high (hi). set time to 22 minutes.

5. press the start/stop button to begin and when pressure cooking is complete, allow pressure to natural release for about 5 minutes.

6. after 5 minutes cooking time, quick release the pressure by moving the pressure release valve to the vent position.

7. carefully remove lid when unit has finished releasing pressure. Brush chicken with canola oil or spray with cooking spray. season with salt and pepper.

8. Close crisping lid. select air crisp, set temperature to 400°F, and set time to 8 minutes.

9. select start/stop to begin. cook until desired level of crispness is reached, adding up to 10 additional minutes.

10. Allow the chicken rest for about 5 to 10 minutes. cooking is complete when internal temperature reaches 165°F.

11. Remove chicken from basket using the ninja roast lifters. Serve immediately and Enjoy!

FISH AND SEAFOODS

Fish and Grits

Preparation time: 10 minutes

Cooking time: 28 minutes

Overall time: 38 minutes

Serves: 1 to 3 people

Recipe Ingredients:

- 3 cups of chicken broth
- 1 cup of heavy cream
- 1 cup of stone ground grits
- 2 tablespoons of butter
- 1 teaspoon of salt
- 2 pieces of tilapia fish
- 2 teaspoons of blackened or cajun seasoning
- Vegetable oil in a spray bottle

Cooking Instructions:

1. Place chicken broth, heavy cream, grits, salt and butter in your Ninja Foodi insert.

2. Stir and cover with pressure cooker cover. Make sure valve is set to Seal. Cook on High Pressure for about 8 minutes.

3. Once 8 minutes cooking time is up, allow the Ninja Foodi to naturally release pressure for 10 minutes.

4. Press the cancel button and release the remaining pressure by turning the valve to Vent.

5. Meanwhile, season fish with blackened or Cajun seasoning by first spraying the fish, then rubbing the seasoning into both sides of the fish.

6. Once all pressure is released, open Foodi and stir grits. Place a piece of heavy duty foil on top of the grits to cover.

7. Lay the seasoned fish on top of the foil. Spray again with oil. Close the Air Crisp lid on the ninja Foodi.

8. Cook at 400°F for about 10 minutes or until fish can be easily flaked with a fork. Serve fish over grits and Enjoy

Apricot & Country Mustard Salmon

Preparation time: 5 minutes

Cooking time: 10 minutes

Overall time: 15 minutes

Serves: 2 to 4 people

Recipe Ingredients:

- 2 cups of water
- ¼ cup of apricot preserves
- 2 tbsp. of country
- Dijon-style mustard
- 1½ lb. of salmon fillets
- Salt and ground black pepper

Cooking Instructions:

1. Stir preserves and mustard in bowl and pour 2 cups of water into pot.

2. Season fish with salt and black pepper and place fish on roasting rack, spread preserve mixture on fish.

3. Place rack into pot and set Oven to 400°F for about 20 minutes, checking after 10 to 15 minutes for desired doneness.

4. Serve immediately and Enjoy!

Apricot Preserve Glazed Salmon & Brussel Sprouts with Red Onions

Preparation time: 5 minutes

Cooking time: 25 minutes

Overall time: 30 minutes

Serves: 2 to 4 people

Recipe Ingredients:

- Salmon
- ½ cup Smucker's apricot preserves
- Water
- 2 tablespoons of butter (or Olive oil)
- Red onions, chopped
- Brussel sprouts, halved

Cooking Instructions:

1. Turn your Ninja to 350°F and preheat for about 10 minutes. Place your salmon in your Ninja baking pan and place on the rack.

2. Cook for about 25 minutes. For the glaze, using a small bowl, add a little water to the Smucker's apricot preserves.

3. Once the salmon is done remove it from the baking pan. Pour the apricot mixture in the Ninja baking pan then add the salmon back on top.

4. Cook for a few minutes. Then spoon the glaze over the salmon and serve it up with the Brussel sprouts.

5. While the Salmon is baking, start your 2nd Ninja about 10 minutes after the 1st. Turn to Stove Top High and melt the butter.

6. Add the chopped red onions and sauté for a few minutes. Add the Brussel sprouts and cook until slightly brown, and tender.

7. Serve immediately and Enjoy!

Coconut Curry Salmon with Zucchini Noodles

Preparation time: 5 minutes

Cooking time: 25 minutes

Overall time: 30 minutes

Serves: 3 to 5 people

Recipe Ingredients:

- 2 tbsp. of yellow curry paste
- 1 sweet onion small in size, halved and sliced
- 1 red bell pepper seeded, halved and sliced
- 2 garlic cloves pressed
- 1 (14.5 ounces) can of coconut milk
- 1 dash of fish sauce
- ¾ lb. of salmon skinned, deboned and cut into 2 fillets
- 1 zucchini spiralized

Cooking Instructions:

1. Set the dial on the Ninja to Stove Top High. Allow to preheat for about 3 minutes. While the unit preheats, prepare the onion.

2. When the cooker is hot enough, add the yellow curry paste and onions. Stir the onions around with a wooden spoon to coat them with the curry.

3. Allow to cook for about 5 minutes. While the onion is cooking, prepare the bell pepper and garlic, as well as the salmon if you haven't already.

4. Add the bell pepper and garlic once the onions are tender, cooking an additional 2 minutes. Pour in the coconut milk and add a dash of fish sauce.

5. Stir to combine. Place the salmon fillets on top of the curry mixture. Place the lid on the cooker and steam for 9 minutes.

6. Spiralizer the zucchini. Once the 9 minutes has completed, open the cooker and place the zucchini delicately on top of the fish.

7. Replace the lid and steam for an additional minute. Turn off the cooker, and remove the lid. Use tongs to remove the zucchini noodles to wide bowls.

8. Place a salmon fillet on top of each mound of zucchini, ladle on the sauce with the onions and bell peppers. Serve and Enjoy!

Crispy Baked Basa (Swai Fish)

Preparation time: 10 minutes

Cooking time: 50 minutes

Overall time: 1 hour

Serves: 3 to 5 people

Recipe Ingredients:

- ¼ cup of mayonnaise
- 1 tbsp. of stone ground mustard
- 1 tsp. of ketchup
- ¼ tsp. of paprika
- ¼ tsp. of hot pepper sauce
- 1 lb. of swai fish
- 1½ tbsp. of olive oil
- 1 cup of finely crushed Ritz Crackers, Panko crumbs, crushed croutons,
- Salt and pepper to taste
- 1 clove of garlic, minced
- 1 lemon, sliced (optional)

Cooking Instructions:

1. Turn your Ninja to the Oven setting of 375°F to begin preheating the Ninja while preparing your ingredients.

2. In a bowl, thoroughly blend the mayonnaise, mustard, ketchup, paprika, and hot pepper sauce.

3. Dip the fish in the sauce instead of olive oil then in bread crumbs-so the fish was cooked with the sauce right on it.

4. Season the fish with salt, pepper and garlic powder. Arrange the fish in the multipurpose pan and top with garlic and lemon slices.

5. Place the rack in the Ninja pot and place the pan. Bake for about 30 minutes. These baked up with a nice coating that were pretty crispy.

6. Use of ¼ cup of mayonnaise and bake for about 30-minutes total time for the fish to be flaky.

7. Serve immediately and Enjoy!

Fish Cakes

Preparation time: 5 minutes

Cooking time: 10 minutes

Overall time: 15 minutes

Serves: 2 to 4 people

Recipe Ingredients:

- 2 servings of cooked fish
- 1-2 carrots (depending on size)
- 1-2 stalks of celery
- Small onion
- ½ cup of soft bread crumbs
- 2 eggs
- Handful of fresh herbs, dried are fine too
- ¼ teaspoon of seafood seasoning
- 1 teaspoon of turmeric
- 1 teaspoon of pepper and season salt
- Chives
- ½ teaspoon of salt

Cooking Instructions:

1. Put the veggies in a food processor and mince. Remove the minced veggies and put the fish and fresh herbs in and mince.

2. Combined the fish and vegetables in a bowl add the spices, stir well. Add the bread crumbs, mix well.

3. Add the eggs one at a time- you may need just one to bind the mixture. Form into 6 cakes and heat the Ninja to Stove Top High.

4. Add 1 tablespoon of olive oil. Once the oil is hot, add three patties to the Ninja pot. Brown patties on both sides. Repeat with the remaining cakes.

5. Serve immediately and Enjoy!

Indian Style Shrimp

Preparation time: 5 minutes

Cooking time: 10 minutes

Overall time: 15 minutes

Serves: 3 to 5 people

Recipe Ingredients:

- 1 tbsp. of olive oil
- 1 onion, chopped
- 1 heaping tablespoon of minced garlic
- 2 lb. of peeled and cleaned shrimp
- 48 oz. can of crushed tomatoes, (or more if desired)
- 1 tsp. of cayenne pepper
- 1 tsp. curry powder
- 1 tsp. ground powder ginger
- 2 tsp. parsley flakes
- 1 tsp. garlic powder
- 2 tsp. salt
- 2 packets of Splenda or one tablespoon sugar
- 1 cup of sour cream
- Flour or corn starch slurry, (optional for thickening)

Cooking Instructions:

1. Turn the Ninja to Stove Top High. Add the olive oil and sauté onion and garlic and add shrimp. Try to leave shrimp a little under cooked.

2. Remove them from the pot. Add crushed tomatoes, cayenne pepper, curry, ginger, parsley flakes, garlic powder, salt, and Splenda or sugar.

3. Cook until bubbling hot, return the shrimp and stir in sour cream depending on how creamy you want it.

4. Turn to the Oven setting of 425°F for about 10 minutes. Adjust any seasonings you prefer. for a thicker consistency just add in a flour or corn starch slurry.

5. Serve immediately and Enjoy!

Lobster with Fried Rice

Preparation time: 5 minutes

Cooking time: 5 minutes

Overall time: 10 minutes

Serves: 2 to 4 people

Recipe Ingredients:

- 3 cups of cooked rice
- 2 tablespoons of sesame oil
- 1 small white onion, chopped
- 1 cup of frozen peas
- 7 mini carrots chopped
- 3 tablespoons of soy sauce
- 2 eggs, lightly beaten
- 2 tablespoons of chopped green onions (optional)

Cooking Instructions:

1. Preheat a Ninja to Stove Top High and pour sesame oil in the bottom.

2. Add white onion and carrots and fry until tender and add frozen peas. Slide the onion, peas and carrots to the side, and pour the beaten eggs onto the other side.

3. Using a spatula, scramble the eggs. Once cooked, mix the eggs with the vegetable mix. Add the rice to the veggie and egg mixture.

4. Pour the soy sauce on top and stir and fry the rice and veggie mixture until heated through and combined.

5. Stir & switched to warm after about 2 minutes. Add chopped green onions if desired.

6. Cook rice in the morning or night before and refrigerate & then use in this recipe. You can add some leftover cooked broccoli.

7. Served it with homemade yum-yum sauce.

Maple Salmon

Preparation time: 5 minutes

Cooking time: 50 minutes

Overall time: 55 minutes

Serves: 2 to 4 people

Recipe Ingredients:

- 24 ounces of salmon
- 6 tbsp. of real maple syrup
- 3 tbsp. of soy sauce
- 1 clove of garlic
- ¼ tsp. of garlic salt
- 1/8 tsp. of ground black pepper
- (Optional) pinch of salt since

Cooking Instructions:

1. In a small bowl, mix all the ingredients except salmon.

2. Place salmon in shallow baking dish & cover with maple syrup mixture. Cover the dish & marinate salmon in the refrigerator for about 30 minutes, turning once.

3. Turn on your Ninja to the Oven setting of 400°F and add 2 cups of water to the pot and cover the rack with foil; place the rack in the Ninja.

4. Place the salmon on the rack; cook for about 25 minutes or until it easily flakes with a fork.

5. Serve immediately and Enjoy!

Shrimp Fra Diavolo Over Angel Hair

Preparation time: 5 minutes

Cooking time: 30 minutes

Overall time: 35 minutes

Serves: 2 to 4 people

Recipe Ingredients:

- 12 ounces of raw medium shrimp, peeled, deveined and tail removed
- 12 ounces of angel hair pasta
- 1 tsp. of salt
- 1 tbsp. of dried crushed red pepper flakes
- Olive oil
- 1 medium onion, sliced
- 1 (14.5 oz.) can of diced tomatoes
- 1 (8 oz.) can of tomato sauce
- 1 tbsp. of tomato paste
- 1 cup of dry white wine
- 4 garlic cloves, minced
- 1 tsp. of dried oregano
- ½ cup of chopped fresh parsley
- ¼ cup of chopped fresh basil

Cooking Instructions:

1. Toss the shrimp in a bowl with 1 teaspoon of salt and red pepper flakes. Turn your Ninja 3-in-1 on to Stove Top High and heat approximately 3 tablespoons olive oil.

2. Add the shrimp and sauté for about a minute, toss, and continue cooking until just cooked through, for about 1 to 2 minutes.

3. Transfer the shrimp to a bowl and set it aside. Add the onion to the Ninja pot, adding 2 tablespoons of olive oil, salt and pepper and a big pinch of sugar.

4. Stir frequently sauté for about 10 minutes or so until nicely caramelized. Once the onions are almost done, add the garlic.

5. When the onions are golden, add the tomatoes with their juices, wine, tomato sauce, tomato paste, and oregano.

6. Set the Ninja to Stove Top Low, cover and simmer until the sauce thickens slightly, for about 20 to 30 minutes.

7. When the pasta water is boiling and you've added your pasta and that's cooking away merrily.

8. It would be a good time to return the shrimp, basil and parsley to the sauce and stir well.

9. When the angel hair was done cooking. Serve immediately and Enjoy!

Tortilla Crusted Tilapia

Preparation time: 5 minutes

Cooking time: 30 minutes

Overall time: 35 minutes

Serves: 2 to 4 people

Recipe Ingredients:

- 6 ounces of tortilla chip strips, approximately
- 3 teaspoons of lime juice
- ¼ teaspoon of cayenne pepper
- ¼ cup of cilantro
- ½ teaspoon of chili powder
- 1/8 teaspoon of cumin
- 1 teaspoon of sea salt
- 1 tablespoon of butter, melted
- 4 to 6 tilapia filets
- Flour
- 1 egg

Cooking Instructions:

1. Preheat your Ninja to 375°F with the pyramid mat. In a food processor pulse tortilla strips.

2. Add pepper, lime juice, cilantro, chili powder, cumin, sea salt and melted butter. Pulse until mixed and pour onto a plate.

3. Put flour on another plate, in a bowl beat egg until mixed. Place filets in flour to coat, then put into egg to coat.

4. Finally, coat filets with chip coating. To bake now, put them in the Ninja on a pyramid mat and bake for about 20 minutes.

5. Put additional lime juice on towards the end of baking as well and raised temperature to 400°F for the last 5 minutes.

6. Serve immediately and Enjoy!

Tilapia Filets

Preparation time: 5 minutes

Cooking time: 20 minutes

Overall time: 25 minutes

Serves: 2 to 4 people

Recipe Ingredients:

- Tilapia filets
- Salt and pepper
- Garlic powder
- Season salt
- Adobo
- Old Bay
- Butter
- Lemon
- White wine
- 4 cups of water
- Minute rice
- Frozen peas

Cooking Instructions:

1. Use the Ninja baking pan with the rack to make fish. Get the tilapia filets and season with salt, pepper, garlic powder, season salt, Adobo, and Old Bay.

2. Then put pat of butter and lemon slices on each one and drizzle with a good dry white wine or something you will drink.

3. Put 4 cups of water in bottom of the Ninja, 1½ cups minute rice, salt, and pepper. Put the rack inside the Ninja, then the pan.

4. Turn to Oven setting of 375°F for about 20 minutes. The last few minutes add frozen peas to the rice.

5. When the fish flakes apart, remove and add to tablespoons of butter to the rice. Stir and enjoy.

Swordfish with Aloha Rice & Vegetables

Preparation time: 10 minutes

Cooking time: 60 minutes

Overall time: 1 hour 10 minutes

Serves: 3 to 5 people

Recipe Ingredients:

- 1 cup of long grain brown rice, uncooked
- 1 cup of chicken stock
- 3 cups of water
- 1 (8 oz.) can of crushed pineapple, with liquid
- ½ cup of green bell pepper, diced
- ½ cup of onion, diced
- 1 tbsp. of soy sauce, (liquid aminos is a suitable substitute)
- 1 tbsp. of honey
- 1 tbsp. of apple cider vinegar
- 1 tsp. of ground ginger
- 1 tsp. of garlic powder
- 1/8 tsp. of crushed red pepper
- 3 carrots, peeled and cut into 2-inch chunks
- 1 cup of broccoli florets
- 2 (3 oz.) swordfish steaks
- 1 tsp. of sesame seeds
- Sea salt and freshly ground black pepper, to taste

Cooking Instructions:

1. Rinse the brown rice in 2-3 changes of water using a strainer.

2. Place the rice, chicken stock and 3 cups water in the Ninja pot and set the dial to Stove Top High.

3. Bring to a boil which takes approximately 10 minutes, turn the dial to Stove Top Medium/Low. Place the lid on the cooker and cook for about 20 minutes.

4. In the meantime, combine the pineapple, green bell pepper, onion, soy sauce, honey, vinegar, ginger, garlic powder and crushed red pepper in a bowl.

5. Stir to combine. You may also use this time to prep the carrots and broccoli if necessary. After the rice has cooked initially for about 20 minutes, open the cooker.

6. Pour in the pineapple mixture and stir to combine with rice. Replace the lid, and cook another 15 minutes. Open the cooker and insert the roasting rack.

7. Place the carrots and swordfish steaks on top of the rack. Sprinkle sesame seeds, salt and pepper over vegetables and fish.

8. Replace the lid and continue cooking covered for 10 minutes. Open the cooker. Add broccoli and cook another 5 minutes.

9. Turn off the cooker and remove the rack with the swordfish and vegetables. Scoop rice onto a plate and serve topped with swordfish and vegetables.

Steamer Clams

Preparation time: 5 minutes

Cooking time: 10 minutes

Overall time: 15 minutes

Serves: 2 to 4 people

Recipe Ingredients:

- 2 lb. of clams
- 1 cup of white dry wine
- 2 tbsp. of vegetable or olive oil
- Half a yellow onion, diced
- 5 garlic cloves, minced
- 4 cups of water
- 2 tsp. of sea salt

Cooking Instructions:

1. Place pot in cooking system and plug the unit into an electrical outlet.

2. Turn the stove top dial to medium. Add oil, onions, garlic and wine. Sauté for about 6 minutes, stirring occasionally.

3. Add water, sea salt, place roasting rack on top of the onion, water & wine mixture. Place clams inside the roasting rack.

4. Place the lid on top of the Ninja and set dial to Oven 425°F and steam for about 7 minutes.

5. Lift roasting rack out, lean sideways and pour the steamers in the broth. Toss to coat, remove then serve!

Shrimp Scampi

Preparation time: 10 minutes

Cooking time: 30 minutes

Overall time: 40 minutes

Serves: 3 to 4 people

Recipe Ingredients:

- 4 tbsp. of butter
- 4 cloves of garlic, minced
- ¼ tsp. of crushed red pepper
- 1 cup of chopped fresh parsley
- Salt and ground black pepper
- ½ cup of dry white wine
- 4 cups of water
- 1 package (1 lb.) of angel hair pasta, broken in half
- 1 lb. of frozen cooked, peeled and deveined medium shrimp

Cooking Instructions:

1. Place butter into pot and set to Stove Top High and heat until butter is melted.

2. Stir in garlic, red peppers, half the parsley, salt and black pepper into the pot. Cook uncovered 5 minutes or until garlic is lightly browned, stirring occasionally.

3. Add wine, water and pasta to pot. Stir to submerge pasta in liquid. Set Oven to 300°F for about 15 minutes, checking after 10 minutes.

4. Cover, cook and add shrimp into pot. Set time for another 10 minutes, cover and cook until pasta is tender and shrimp are heated through.

5. Sprinkle with remaining parsley and serve.

VEGERARIAN RECIPE

Cabbage Rolls

Preparation time: 10 minutes

Cooking time: 40 minutes

Overall time: 5 0 minutes

Serves: 2 to 4 people

Recipe Ingredients:

- 1 whole cabbage, chopped
- 1½ cups of wild rice
- 1 large carrot, chopped small
- ½ onion, chopped small
- 5 cloves of garlic, minced
- 2 cans of tomato sauce
- 1 can of tomato soup
- 4 cups of vegetable stock
- Salt and pepper to taste

Cooking Instructions:

1. Add all ingredients to the Ninja and turn to Stove top High and bring to a boil. Reduce heat to Stove Top Low.

2. Cover and cook for about 45 to 50 minutes or until rice is done and cabbage becomes soft.

3. Serve immediately and Enjoy!

Ratatouille

Preparation time: 10 minutes

Cooking time: 4 hours

Overall time: 4 hours 10 minutes

Serves: 2 to 4 people

Recipe Ingredients:

- 2 tablespoons of olive oil
- 3 cloves of garlic, sliced
- 1 medium size onion, chopped
- 1 eggplant
- 2 zucchinis, chopped in cubes
- 2 red peppers, sliced in strips
- 1 (28 ounces) can of diced tomatoes
- Salt, pepper and a touch of oregano
- ¼ cup (around that amount) of basil
- Tomato paste to thicken

Cooking Instructions:

1. Sauté the onion in the olive oil on Stove Top High until tender and add garlic, peppers, eggplant, and zucchini to crock.

2. Cook for about 5 to 10 minutes until a bit tender; but still a bit crisp. Add the tomatoes, & spices (except the basil). \

3. Stir and Slow Cook Low for 4 hours. About ½ hour before done, when veggies are now tender, add the basil.

4. Serve immediately and Enjoy!

Spicy Black Bean Burgers

Preparation time: 20 minutes

Cooking time: 2 hours

Overall time:2 hours 20 minutes

Serves: 2 to 4 people

Recipe Ingredients:

- 1 white onion
- 3 jalapeno peppers (keep or remove seed) or 15 marinated jalepeno slices
- 3 garlic cloves
- 2- 14.5 ounces cans black beans - drained
- 1 cup rolled instant oats
- 15 oz can corn - drained
- 2 scallion stalks
- salt - to taste
- ground black pepper - to taste
- chili powder - to taste
- 4 burger buns

Cooking Instructions:

1. Make the mix for the burgers 2 hours before making them as it needs to be refrigerated for at least two hours.

2. Use a food processor to make the burger mix. Into the food processor, add the onion, jalapeno and garlic and pulse 9 or 10 times.

3. Add the beans, oats, corn, scallions, chili powder, salt, and ground black pepper and pulse until you teach your desired texture/consistency.

4. Transfer the mixture to a bowl, make sure to seal tightly with plastic wrap or just put a lid on your food processor and put it into the fridge for at least 2 hours.

5. Add a splash of olive oil to the Ninja pot. Divide and make 4 balls of black bean mixture.

6. Add to the pot, then press them down to give them the patty appearance. Turn the Ninja to Stove Top High and place the lid on the Ninja.

7. Cook each side for about 10 to 13 minutes or until you see that each side has solidified and browned. On a bun with vegetables as a garnish, or eat as is.

Tamale Pie

Preparation time: 10 minutes

Cooking time: 50 minutes

Overall time: 1 hour

Serves: 3 to 5 people

Recipe Ingredients:

For topping:

- 1 pouch cornbread & muffin mix (used Betty Crocker's)
- ¼ cup fat free liquid egg substitute
- 3 Tbs. no sugar applesauce

For Pie:

- 12 oz package Morning Star Farms Crumbles
- ½ cup canned sweet corn, drained
- ½ cup black beans
- 1/3 cup chopped onion (I added a whole onion)
- 2 Tbs. taco sauce (I use ¼ cup green taco sauce)
- 1 tsp taco seasoning (I used 2 tsp Ortega)
- ½ tsp ground cumin (I used 1 tsp)

Directions:

1. Mix together cornbread, egg sub & applesauce and set it aside.

2. Lightly spray Ninja pot with Pam, once pan is heated cook onion & crumbles until crumbles are thawed.

3. Add in taco seasoning, cumin & ¼ cup of water, stirring occasionally until water absorbed for about 2 minutes.

4. Add taco sauce, corn and black beans, mix well and cook covered on skillet high for about 6 to 8 minutes, stir every 4 minutes.

5. Remove lid and if still a bit runny looking, cook another 2 minutes or so uncovered. Spray pan that will fit in Ninja with Pam and spoon meat mixture into it.

6. Spread cornbread mixture on top of meat. Carefully lift out Ninja pot and rinse well, dry and put back in Ninja.

7. Add 2½ cups of water to bottom of Ninja, add rack. Place pan with pie in it on rack, cover and bake at 350°F for about 20 to 25 minutes.

8. Check at 20 minutes to see if the cornbread had risen or brown. Do a toothpick test and covered again for another 4 minutes.

9. Added a couple of heaping spoonsful to my little bowl and added some green taco sauce, it is very, very good.

10. Serve immediately and Enjoy!

Tuscan Soup

Preparation time: 5 minutes

Cooking time: 10 minutes

Overall time: 15 minutes

Serves: 2 to 4 people

Recipe Ingredients:

- 4 ounces of vegetarian sausage, crumbled or minced
- 2 tablespoons of extra virgin olive oil
- ½ red or yellow onion, diced
- 1 teaspoon of fresh minced or dried minced garlic, reconstituted and drained
- ¼ teaspoon of salt
- Pinch crushed red pepper
- 1 teaspoon of dried Italian herb blend
- 3 cups of vegetable broth
- 1 bunch kale, stems removed and chopped
- ½ cup of heavy cream
- Fresh ground black pepper

Cooking Instructions:

1. Heat olive oil in Ninja on stove top medium. Sauté onion, stirring, until almost translucent.

2. Add sausage and continue to cook for about 4 minutes. Turn down to Stove Top Low and add garlic. Stir for about 2 minutes.

3. Add Italian herbs, salt, and crushed red pepper and stir. Add broth and stir, heat on Stove Top High until boiling.

4. Then turn back down to stove top low and cover. Leave for a few minutes to blend the flavors.

5. Stir kale into soup ½ an hour before you plan to serve it. About 5 minutes before serving time, stir in heavy cream. Just before serving,

6. Add a few grinds of fresh ground black pepper, serve

Vegetarian Chili

Preparation time: 5 minutes

Cooking time: 5 minutes

Overall time: 10 minutes

Serves: 2 to 4 people

Recipe Ingredients:

- 1 tbsp. of olive oil
- ½ medium onion, chopped
- 2 bay leaves
- 1 teaspoon of cumin
- 2 tbsp. of dried oregano
- 1 tbsp. of salt
- 2 stalks celery, chopped
- 2 green bell peppers, chopped
- 2 jalapeno peppers, chopped
- 3 gloves of garlic
- 2 (4 ounces) cans of green chile peppers, drained
- 2 (12 ounces) packages of veggie burger crumbles
- 3 (28 ounces) whole peeled tomatoes crushed
- ¼ cup of chili powder
- 1 tbsp. of black pepper
- 1 (15 ounces) kidney beans, drained
- 1 (15 ounces) garbanzo beans, drained
- 1 (15 ounces) black beans, drained
- 1 (15 ounces) whole kernel, corn

Cooking Instructions:

1. Heat the olive oil over medium heat (low in 4–in–1). Stir in the onion and season with bay leaves, cumin, oregano and salt.

2. Cook and stir until onion is tender, then mix in celery, green bell peppers, jalapeno peppers, garlic and green chile peppers.

3. When veggies are heated, turn Ninja to Stove Top High. Mix in the veggie crumbles and add the tomatoes and corn into the pot.

4. Season with chili powder and pepper and stir in all the beans. Turn to Slow Cook Low and let the flavors come together for about 2 hours, or longer.

5. The Ninja will switch to Auto Warm to hold. Remove bay leaf and serve with shredded cheese, sour cream.

Vegetarian Meatloaf

Preparation time: 10 minutes

Cooking time: 50 minutes

Overall time: 1 hour

Serves: 3 to 5 people

Recipe Ingredients:

- 1 tablespoon of Vegetable oil
- ½ carrot
- Half a stick of celery
- Half an onion
- 2 cloves of garlic
- ¼ red or green or yellow pepper

Topping:

- 3 tablespoons of ketchup
- 1 teaspoons of soft brown sugar
- ¼ teaspoon made mustard
- Splash of Worcestershire sauce
- Sweet chili sauce

Cooking Instructions:

1. To a bowl add 500gms of vegetarian mince. the onion, 1 tablespoon of dried Oregano.

2. A generous amount of ground pepper and salt. Big splash of Worcestershire sauce1 cup of breadcrumbs, chopped fresh parsley (lots)2 eggs

3. Put the carrot, celery, onion, garlic & pepper in a food processor and pulse about 4 or 5 times.

4. Do not puree them, add the oil to a frying pan and add the mix. Add generous seasoning, a good splash of Worcester sauce and fry it for about 7 minutes.

5. Allow it to cool. Pre-heat Ninja to oven 375°F and mix your ketchup, soft brown sugar, made mustard, splash of Worcestershire sauce and sweet chili sauce

6. Grease your loaf tin, add mixture and flatten it down. Spread on topping, place loaf tin on roasting rack and lower it in the Ninja.

7. Cook it for about 45 minutes, apply more topping every 20 minutes or so. Take it out and let it cool for about 10 minutes before trying to get it out of the tin.

8. Served it in slices with potato salad and coleslaw.

Vegetarian Moroccan Red Lentil Soup or Stew

Preparation time: 5 minutes

Cooking time: 5 minutes

Overall time: 10 minutes

Serves: 2 to 4 people

Recipe Ingredients:

- 2 tablespoons of olive oil
- 2 large onions, medium dice
- 2 cloves of garlic, minced
- 1 teaspoon of fresh ginger
- 1 package of tempeh
- 2 teaspoons of ground coriander
- 1 teaspoon of ground cumin
- 1 teaspoon of ground turmeric
- ¼ teaspoon of cinnamon
- Salt to taste
- ½ teaspoon of black pepper
- 7 cups of vegetable broth
- 1 can of crushed tomatoes
- 1 jar of ethnic cottage punjab spinach cooking sauce - optional
- 2 cups of dry red lentils
- Juice of 1 lemon
- Parsley and cilantro - to taste

Cooking Instructions:

1. Turn the Ninja to Stove Top High and add the oil and saute onions and garlic.

2. Add all spices and tempeh. Stir well for a minute and add broth and tomatoes. Heat to a boil. Wash and drain the lentils. Stir in the lentils, carrots and kale.

3. Reduce the heat to Stove Top Low for 1 hour. Stir occasionally during that time. You may need to add additional broth if you add a lot of vegetables.

4. Serve immediately and Enjoy!

Vegetarian Ninja Jambalaya Pasta Soup

Preparation time: 5 minutes

Cooking time: 5 minutes

Overall time: 10 minutes

Serves: 2 to 4 people

Recipe Ingredients:

- 2 tablespoons of peanut oil
- ½ red onion, chopped
- Small amount of red bell pepper, chopped
- 1 or 2 meatless Italian sausages, sliced into rounds
- 1 teaspoons of dried minced garlic, reconstituted in water
- 1 teaspoon of Essence powdered seasoning
- 1 teaspoon of Cajun seasoning
- 3 cups of No-Chicken broth
- 1 cup of bow ties or other small pasta, uncooked
- ¼ cup of heavy cream

Cooking Instructions:

1. Sauté onion and red pepper in the oil in Ninja on Stove Top Medium. When it is nearly tender, add sliced sausages and continue to sauté.

2. In 2 or 3 minutes, add the garlic, drained, and the two seasonings and cook, stirring, until garlic looks cooked but not browned.

3. Then add the broth and turn to Stove Top High, covering the Ninja with the lid to make it boil faster.

4. When the broth boils, turn the Ninja to Stove Top Low and add the pasta and cook, covered.

5. When the pasta is tender, add the cream. Stir and serve. Delicious!

Mushroom Tofu Ramen

Preparation time: 5 minutes

Cooking time: 30 minutes

Overall time: 35 minutes

Serves: 2 to 4 people

Recipe Ingredients:

Tofu:

- 1 (16 ounces) of block extra firm tofu
- 2 tablespoons of olive oil
- Salt
- pepper

Ramen:

- 4 cups of vegetable broth
- 1 tablespoon of minced ginger
- 2 cloves of garlic, crushed
- 8 ounces of baby bella mushrooms, sliced
- 1 (1 ounces) package dried Shitake mushrooms
- 2 cups of water
- 1 package of Ramen Noodles, flavor packet discarded
- ¼ cup of green onion
- 2 Marinated Soft Boiled Eggs
- Black sesame seeds, for garnish

Cooking Instructions:

1. Press the tofu to release any excess water, slice tofu into 1-inch cubes. In a medium sized bowl, toss the tofu cubes in olive oil and season with salt and pepper.

2. Turn Ninja Foodie on "Air Crisp" function, preheat for about 5 minutes at 400°F. Spray the crisper basket with non-stick spray.

3. Place tofu in the basket, crisp for about 15 minutes, tossing the tofu every 5 minutes so it crisps evenly. When tofu is done, remove the basket and set it aside.

4. Switch your Ninja Foodie to the Pressure function and pour the vegetable broth and mix in the ginger. Add the garlic and mushrooms.

5. Seal the pot with the pressure cook lid, make sure the pressure valve is set to seal, cook for about 10 minutes at high pressure.

6. Use natural release method to release the pressure, when it is safe to do so, open the lid and dd 2 cups of water.

7. Switch to the "sear/sauté" function, liquid will quickly come to a boil, add the Ramen Noodles, cook for about 3 minutes.

8. Carefully remove the pot from the Ninja Foodie. Divide the broth and noodles into 2 large soup bowls.

9. Top each with a generous amount of tofu, green onions, 1 halved Marinated Soft Boiled Egg and a sprinkle of black sesame seeds. Enjoy immediately

SIDE DISHES AND APPETIZERS

Bacon Wrapped Smokies

Preparation time: 5 minutes

Cooking time: 25 minutes

Overall time: 30 minutes

Serves: 2 to 4 people

Recipe Ingredients:

- 1 lb. of little smoky sausages
- 1 lb. of maple bacon
- ¾ cup of brown sugar

Cooking Instructions:

1. Cut bacon into thirds. Wrap each smoky with a third of a strip of bacon and fasten with tooth pick.

2. Line the bottom of Ninja with the wrapped smokies. Sprinkle the brown sugar on top.

3. Cook on Oven setting at 325°F for about 30 minutes, check to see if you need 10 minutes more, or until the bacon is crisped.

4. Serve from the Ninja on Buffet setting.

Barbequed Wings

Preparation time: 10 minutes

Cooking time: 3 hours

Overall time: 3 hours 10 minutes

Serves: 3 to 5 people

Recipe Ingredients:

- Wings
- 1¼ cups of ketchup
- 1 cup of dark brown sugar
- ¼ cup of molasses
- ¼ cup of pineapple juice or apple cider vinegar
- ¼ cup of water
- 1 tablespoon of Worcestershire sauce
- 2½ teaspoons of ground mustard
- 2 teaspoons of smoked paprika
- ½ teaspoon of garlic powder
- ¼ -½ teaspoon of cayenne pepper
- 1½ teaspoons of salt
- 1 teaspoon of pepper

Cooking Instructions:

1. Turn the Ninja to Stove Top High and brown the wings on both sides for about 5 minutes each.

2. Combine ingredients in medium size sauce pot. Bring to boil and reduce and simmer for five minutes or until sugar has dissolved.

3. When the wings are finished browning, coat them with the sauce. Return them to the Ninja.

4. Turn to Slow Cook Low for about 3 hours. They were fall off the bone delicious, checking at 2 ½ hours.

5. Serve immediately and Enjoy!

Black-Eyed Pea Cheese Dip

Preparation time: 5 minutes

Cooking time: 5 minutes

Overall time: 10 minutes

Serves: 6 to 8 people

Recipe Ingredients:

- ½ lb. of ground sausage
- 1 medium onion, finely chopped
- 4 cloves of garlic, finely chopped
- 15 ounces of can of black-eyed peas, drained
- 10 ounces can of Ro*Tel
- 1 teaspoon of chipotle chili powder
- 1 lb. of Velveeta, cut into 1-inch cubes
- Chips for serving

Cooking Instructions:

1. Turn the Ninja to Stove Top High and add crumbled sausage and begin browning.

2. Add the onion and garlic with the sausage. Drain any grease if necessary. Stir in black eyed peas, Ro*Tel and chili powder.

3. Add cheese and stir as needed. Reduce the heat to Stove Top Low to melt the cheese.

4. Serve with chips and Enjoy!

Buffalo Chicken Dip

Preparation time: 5 minutes

Cooking time: 5 minutes

Overall time: 10 minutes

Serves: 2 to 4 people

Recipe Ingredients:

- 2 lb. of chicken cut in cubes
- 4 cups of shredded cheddar cheese
- 5-ounces packages of light cream cheese,
- 1 (12 ounces) small jar of blue cheese dressing
- 2 cups of hot sauce or any you like, (to taste)
- Crumbled blue cheese, optional

Cooking Instructions:

1. Turn the Ninja to Stove Top High and cook the chicken.

2. Add the cheddar cheese, cream cheese, blue cheese, and hot sauce. Melt, still using the Stove Top setting.

3. Once all is melted turn to Slow Cook Low for about 1-2 hours or longer. Switch to Buffet setting to keep hot for serving.

4. Use as a dip for tortilla chips, celery, pita chips etc. serve immediately and Enjoy!

Caprese Bruschetta

Preparation time: 5 minutes

Cooking time: 15 minutes

Overall time: 20 minutes

Serves: 2 to 4 people

Recipe Ingredients:

- 8 oz. of balsamic vinegar
- 8 oz. of fresh mozzarella
- 2 tbsp. of fresh chopped basil
- 2 cups of cherry tomatoes
- 1 French baguette loaf

Cooking Instructions:

1. Pour the balsamic vinegar into a small saucepan and heat over low to medium heat until it comes to a slow boil. Allow to simmer for about 8-10 minutes.

2. The vinegar will thicken while it cooks. Once the amount that is in the pan reduces by about half, turn the heat off.

3. Pour the vinegar into a bowl and allow to cool. As the vinegar cools it will thicken more and become a glaze.

4. Chop the fresh mozzarella and cut the cherry tomatoes in half or thirds to desired size.

5. Roll the basil to chop into fine strips. Combine the mozzarella, tomatoes, and basil together and gently stir to mix.

6. Slice the baguette into desired slice size. You can toast the baguette if desired, or serve un-toasted.

7. To toast, preheat your Ninja to 400°F. Wrap aluminum foil around the rack. Lay the slices down on the foil and cover with butter or olive oil.

8. Bake for about 8 to 10 minutes until it is golden brown. Serve with the bruschetta on top of the baguette and a balsamic glaze drizzle on top.

Cashew Caramel Corn

Preparation time: 5 minutes

Cooking time: 20 minutes

Overall time: 25 minutes

Serves: 3 to 5 people

Recipe Ingredients:

- 1 cup of unsalted butter
- 2 cup of brown sugar
- ½ cup of light corn syrup
- ½ teaspoon of salt
- ½ teaspoon of baking soda
- 1 teaspoon of vanilla extract
- 2 cup of raw unsalted, unroasted whole cashews
- 4 quarts popped popcorn

Cooking Instructions:

1. Preheat Ninja on Stove Top High for about 7 minutes. Melt the butter in the pot. Stir in brown sugar, syrup, and salt; bring mixture to a boil.

2. Stir and once combined continue to boil without stirring for about 3 to 4 minutes. When mixture starts to bubble, turn the Ninja to the Oven setting of 250°F.

3. Stir in the baking soda and vanilla, mix well and then immediately add the cooked popcorn and cashews.

4. Stir continuously until both popcorn and nuts and evenly coated, for about 3 minutes.

5. Put on the lid and bake for about 15 minutes; stirring every 5 minutes or so. Empty the warm popcorn mixture on a sheet of paper in a single layer.

6. Once it has fully cooled break it apart and store in an airtight container. Melt some milk chocolate in the Ninja.

7. Then pour it over the caramel corn when it is cooling. Let the chocolate harden before storing it.

Chex Mix

Preparation time: 10 minutes

Cooking time: 2 hours

Overall time: 2 hours 10 minutes

Serves: 2 to 4 people

Recipe Ingredients:

- 3 cups of corn Chex cereal
- 3 cups of rice Chex cereal
- 3 cups of wheat Chex cereal
- 3 cups of cheerios cereal
- 3 cups of pretzel sticks
- 1 can (10.3 ounces) mixed nuts
- 1 cup of melted butter
- 2 tbsp. of Worcestershire sauce
- 1 ½ tsp. of seasoned salt
- ¾ tsp. of garlic powder

Cooking Instructions:

1. Mix all three Chex cereals, Cheerios cereal, pretzel sticks, and mixed nuts in your Ninja.

2. Whisk together butter, Worcestershire sauce, seasoned salt and garlic powder and pour over cereal mixture and mix well.

3. Cook on Slow Cook Low for about 2 1/2 hours, stirring frequently, (about every 20 minutes).

4. Add the lid, Turn the lid so it does not sit flush. Spread on a cookie sheet to cool. Measure cereals, nuts and pretzels in to my very large Tupperware Bowl.

5. Place the lid and rotate to mix. Melt the butter. Add Worcestershire sauce, seasoned salt and garlic powder.

6. Stir. Remove part of the cereal mixture and pour half of the butter mix. Place the lid and rotate.

7. Add the rest of the cereal and butter mixture. Place lid and rotate to mix. Pour into the Ninja. Serve immediately and Enjoy!

Chili Dip

Preparation time: 5 minutes

Cooking time: 55 minutes

Overall time: 1 hour

Serves: 2 to 4 people

Recipe Ingredients:

- 2 pounds of ground beef
- 1 onion, diced
- 3 tablespoons of chili powder
- 1 (24 ounces) bottle of ketchup
- Salt and pepper to taste
- Chopped raw onions
- Grated cheddar cheese
- 2 cans of red kidney beans, mashed or blended with juice

Cooking Instructions:

1. Brown meat and onion in the Ninja on Stove Top High. Drain any grease.

2. Add chili powder, ketchup, and mashed or blended kidney beans. Turn to Slow Cook High for about 60 minutes.

3. It will be plenty hot and will go to Auto Warm setting. Serve with chopped raw onions, and grated cheddar cheese.

4. Use your favorite chips for dipping.

Cinnamon Almonds

Preparation time: 20 minutes

Cooking time: 4 hours

Overall time: 4 hours 20 minutes

Serves: 2 to 4 people

Recipe Ingredients:

- 1 ½ cup of sugar
- 1 ½ cup of brown sugar
- 3 tablespoons of cinnamon
- 1/8 tsp. salt
- 1 egg white
- 2 teaspoons of vanilla
- 3 cups almonds
- ¼ cup of water
- PAM cooking spray

Cooking Instructions:

1. In a medium sized bowl, mix together sugars, cinnamon, and salt and set it aside.

2. In another medium sized bowl, whisk the egg white and vanilla until it's a little frothy and add almonds.

3. Make sure the almonds are thoroughly coated in the egg white mixture. Add cinnamon mixture to the almonds and toss until coated.

4. Thoroughly spray the Ninja pot with non-stick cooking spray and add the mixture of almonds and sugars.

5. Cook on Slow Cook Low, for about 3 to 4 hours stirring every 20 minutes. In the last hour, add the ¼ cup of water and stir well.

6. This ensures a crunchy yummy coating. You have to stir really well, especially as it gets later in the cooking process.

7. Line a baking sheet with parchment and spread the almonds flat to cool. The almonds will be sticky at this point.

8. Make sure you separate them a little and have no large mounds. Serve immediately and Enjoy!

Crab Artichoke Bacon Dip

Preparation time: 5 minutes

Cooking time: 20 minutes

Overall time: 25 minutes

Serves: 2 to 4 people

Recipe Ingredients:

- 8 ounces of cream cheese, softened to room temperature
- 1 cup of mayonnaise
- 1 cup of shredded Monterey Jack - to mix in the dip
- ½ cup of shredded Monterey Jack - to top it with before baking
- ½ cup of finely grated Parmesan
- 14 ounces can of artichoke hearts, chopped finely
- ½ pound of bacon, cooked and crumbled
- Kosher salt, to taste
- Freshly ground black pepper, to taste
- 12 ounces of lump crab meat
- 2 green onions, sliced
- 2 teaspoons of Worcestershire sauce
- Hot sauce, a couple of dashes
- 1 baguette, for serving (or crackers, for dipping - your choice)

Recipe Directions:

1. While preparing the dip, turn the Ninja to the Oven setting of 425°F, to begin heating the pot.

2. In a large bowl, combine cream cheese, mayonnaise, 1 cup Monterey Jack, Parmesan, artichokes, bacon, garlic if using, crab meat, green onions, Worcestershire, and hot sauce if using.

3. Season to taste with salt and pepper. Transfer dip to the Ninja multipurpose pan and sprinkle remaining ½ cup of Monterey Jack cheese on top.

4. Place the rack in the Ninja pot. Place the multipurpose pan on rack in Ninja and bake until warmed through and bubbly, for about 25 minutes.

5. Serve warm with baguette slices, toasted or not, your choice. Or crackers.

Light Buffalo Chicken Dip

Preparation time: 10 minutes

Cooking time: 50 minutes

Overall time: 60 minutes

Serves: 2 to 4 people

Recipe Ingredients:

- 16 ounces of Low-Fat Ranch Dressing
- 12 ounces of Hanks Red Hot Sauce
- 8 ounces of cream cheese
- 4 (8 ounces) 98% fat free chunky chicken (canned) - remove liquid
- 2 cups of cheese of choice

Cooking Instructions:

1. Mix hot sauce, ranch dressing, cream cheese, and chicken together then place it in the multipurpose pan or larger oven proof dish.

2. Once in pan, cover it with cheese of choice and place it in the Ninja. Set your Ninja to the Oven mode of 325°F.

3. Bake for about 45 to 60 minutes, or until cheese forms a nice crust. Let cool before serving.

Four Cheese & Onion Dip

Preparation time: 5 minutes

Cooking time: 50 minutes

Overall time: 55 minutes

Serves: 3 to 5 people

Recipe Ingredients:

- 1 cup of shredded cheddar jack cheese
- ½ cup of shredded Swiss cheese
- ¼ cup of grated Parmesan cheese
- 2/3 cup of whipped salad dressing like Miracle Whip (I only use Hellman's)
- 2/3 cup of diced yellow onion
- ½ cup of milk
- ¼ teaspoon of salt

Cooking Instructions:

1. Preheat the Ninja for about 5 to 10 minutes on the Oven setting of 375°F, while preparing dip.

2. Mix together all of the ingredients. Spread into a 1 qt. baking dish. If you have the red silicone rack, place your dish, or use your rack.

3. Bake for about 50 minutes. When done, you can place under the broiler for about 4 to 5 minutes to brown if you like.

4. Serve with whole wheat Ritz crackers, crackers of your choice or vegetable sticks.

Fried Jalapeno Poppers

Preparation time: 5 minutes

Cooking time: 10 minutes

Overall time: 15 minutes

Serves: 2 to 4 people

Recipe Ingredients:

- Jalapeno peppers
- Brick of cream cheese, softened
- Mozzarella cheese, shredded
- Garlic powder
- Buttermilk
- Flour
- Bread crumbs or panko crumbs
- Oil for deep frying
- Rubber gloves

Cooking Instructions:

1. Line a baking sheet with paper towels. Put water in the Ninja pot and begin to heat to boiling.

2. Wear gloves to be safe and slice the jalapenos either in half lengthwise or cut the tops off.

3. Cut the tops off and using a small melon baller scooped out the seeds and ribs, rinse. When the water boils, add the jalapenos and return to boil.

4. Cook until they feet firm, but soft. Drain and plunge into an ice water bath. Remove and place on baking sheet to dry.

5. Using a fork, whip the cream cheese, mozzarella cheese and garlic powder until well blended. Fill peppers.

6. Set aside onto baking sheet again. Pour buttermilk into a bowl, flour into another bowl and bread crumbs yet into another bowl.

7. Dip in buttermilk then in the flour coating completely. Set on the baking sheet again to dry.

8. Then dip back into the buttermilk again and this time roll in bread crumbs. Place on the baking sheet again. Preheat oil in the Ninja.

9. Turn to the Oven setting of 425°F. Once hot, fry the peppers in the hot oil till golden brown.

10. Serve immediately with dipping sauce. Ranch dressing makes a nice dipping sauce.

Gluten-free Caramelized Onion Dip

Preparation time: 15 minutes

Cooking time: 4 hours

Overall time: 4 hours 15 minutes

Serves: 6 to 8 people

Recipe Ingredients:

- 3 cups of chopped onions
- 2 tbsp. of butter
- 6 oz. (12 tbsp.) low fat cream cheese
- 1 cup of part skim mozzarella cheese
- 1/3 cup of soft goat cheese
- 4 tbsp. of low fat mayonnaise
- ½ cup of Chobani plain Greek yogurt (nonfat or 2%)
- Salt and pepper
- Pinch of garlic salt

Cooking Instructions:

1. Turn your Ninja to Stove Top Medium and melt your butter. Add in your onions and heat until fragrant.

2. Reduce the heat to Stove Top Low and cook for about 15 minutes, or until onions are caramelized. Remove onions from pot and place in a bowl.

3. Set the Slow Cook Low and add in salt, pepper, garlic salt, mozzarella cheese, goat cheese, Chobani, mayo and low-fat cream cheese.

4. Heat for about 2 hours, or until mixture is bubbly and gooey. Stir in caramelized onions and heat another 10 to 15 minutes.

5. Serve warm with crackers!

Honey-Glazed Shoyu Chicken Wings

Preparation time: 10 minutes

Cooking time: 40 minutes

Overall time: 50 minutes

Serves: 2 to 4 people

Recipe Ingredients:

- 6 tablespoons of soy sauce
- 1 tablespoon of honey
- 1 tablespoon of sesame oil
- 1 tablespoon of red pepper flakes
- ½ teaspoon of garlic powder
- ½ teaspoon of onion powder

Cooking Instructions:

1. Combine ingredients in a small bowl. Reserve some for brushing on chicken midway through the cooking cycle.

2. Place chicken in a Ziploc bag and pour marinade over chicken. Marinate for one hour.

3. Set Ninja to Oven and the temperature to 350°F. Put the wire rack into the Ninja and pour in 1 cup of water.

4. Place the chicken in a single layer on the rack and steam cook for about 45 minutes. Check to make sure the wings done.

5. After 20 minutes or so, brush wings with the reserved marinade. Serve immediately and Enjoy!

DESSERT RECIPE

Apple Cake

Preparation time: 5 minutes

Cooking time: 2 hours

Overall time: 2 hours 5 minutes

Serves: 2 to 4 people

Recipe Ingredients:

- 2 eggs
- 1¾ cups of sugar
- 2 heaping teaspoons of cinnamon
- ½ cup of oil
- 6 medium apples
- 2 cups of flour
- 2 teaspoon of baking power

Cooking Instructions:

1. Preheat oven to 350°F. Mix the eggs, sugar, cinnamon and oil. Peel and slice the apples and add to mixture in bowl.

2. Mix flour and baking powder and add to the bowl. Mix well until all the flour is absorbed.

3. Pour into your multipurpose pan and place on the rack in the Ninja. Bake on Oven setting of 325°F for about 2hours.

4. Serve immediately and Enjoy!

Baked Custard

Preparation time: 5 minutes

Cooking time: 35 minutes

Overall time: 40 minutes

Serves: 2 to 4 people

Recipe Ingredients:

- 1 Egg
- 1 cup of Milk
- 3 tbsp. of Sugar
- ¾ tsp. of vanilla extract
- 1/8 tsp. of Salt
- 1/8 tsp. of ground nutmeg

Cooking Instructions:

1. In a bowl, lightly beat egg. Add milk, sugar, vanilla and salt. Pour into an ungreased dish.

2. Sprinkle with nutmeg. Set Ninja on Oven setting at 350°F and place custard dish on a low rack, the Ninja rack, or the Pyramid mat.

3. Add hot water to just ½ inch up the side of the dish. Cook for about 40 minutes. The water may boil and splash into the custard a little.

4. Cool and refrigerate.

Baked Rice Pudding

Preparation time: 5 minutes

Cooking time: 20 minutes

Overall time: 25 minutes

Serves: 2 to 4 people

Recipe Ingredients:

- ½ cup of raisins, pit in cool water to soak
- 1 cup of uncooked Carolina rice
- 1½ cups of sugar
- 2 quarts, + 1 pint of milk
- 1 pinch of nutmeg
- 1/8 teaspoon of salt
- ¾ cup of milk
- 2 Eggs
- Cinnamon

Cooking Instructions:

1. Combine above ingredients and "bake" uncovered in 250°F, for about 1 hour.

2. Stir every 10 to 15 minutes to prevent rice from sticking to bottom of Ninja and from scorching on top.

3. Mix and stir into above rice mixture for last 10 minutes of baking. After removing rice pudding.

4. Sprinkle with cinnamon, drain the raisins that have been soaking and add them to the rice pudding. Cool to room temperature and refrigerate.

5. Serve with whipped cream topping.

Black Bean Brownies

Preparation time: 10 minutes

Cooking time: 20 minutes

Overall time: 30 minutes

Serves: 8 to 12 people

Recipe Ingredients:

- ½ cup of canned black beans, rinsed and drained
- ¼ cup of black coffee, strong
- ½ cup of unsalted butter
- 4 ounces of bittersweet chocolate
- 4 large eggs
- 1¼ cups of sugar
- 1 teaspoon of vanilla extract
- 1/8 teaspoon of table salt
- 1 cup of all-purpose flour

Cooking Instructions:

1. Preheat Ninja to 350°F, coat the Ninja pan with cooking spray; & plug the vent with foil.

2. In a blender or mini food processor, process beans with coffee until smooth and set it aside. Melt butter and chocolate in microwave on half power stirring often.

3. Meanwhile, in a medium bowl, using an electric mixer, beat eggs and sugar until light and fluffy.

4. With mixer on low speed, add melted chocolate to eggs; incorporate well. Add black bean mixture, vanilla and salt; mix well.

5. Add flour, combine thoroughly on low speed. Pour batter into prepared pan and bake until a tester inserted in center of brownies comes out clean.

6. Bake for about 20 minutes then unplugged for about 10 minutes before removing to a cooling rack.

7. Top with vanilla ice cream and serve.

Blueberry-Lemon Cake

Preparation time: 10 minutes

Cooking time: 30 minutes

Overall time: 40 minutes

Serves: 2 to 4 people

Recipe Ingredients:

- 2 tablespoons of lemon juice
- 2 tablespoons of grated lemon peel
- 1/3 cup of Splenda brown sugar
- 2 eggs
- 2 tablespoons of coconut oil (or any cooking oil)
- 1 teaspoons of baking powder
- 1 cup of Chobani nonfat plain Greek yogurt
- 1 teaspoon of vanilla
- 2 cups of bisquick baking mix
- PAM cooking spray
- Splenda

Cooking Instructions:

1. In a bowl combine the pint of fresh blueberries, Lemon juice, lemon peel, and brown sugar, stir and let sit.

2. Add the eggs, coconut oil (or any cooking oil), baking powder, yogurt, vanilla, and Bisquick.

3. Pour into pan sprayed with cooking spray. Pour 4 cups of water into the pot. Turn your Ninja to Oven setting of 350°F.

4. Steam bake on rack for about 30 to 40 minutes. Test for doneness. When done I took some regular Splenda white sugar.

5. Put it in a bullet to grind to powder and sprinkled it on top. Serve immediately and Enjoy!

Blueberry Oatmeal Bake

Preparation time: 5 minutes

Cooking time: 40 minutes

Overall time: 45 minutes

Serves: 3 to 5 people

Recipe Ingredients:

- Cooking spray
- ¼ cup of butter melted
- ½ cup of packed brown sugar
- 1 medium egg
- 1 teaspoon of vanilla extract
- ¾ cup of quick oats
- ½ cup of all-purpose flour
- 1/8 teaspoon of salt
- ¾ cup of fresh or frozen blueberries
- 2 cups of water for steaming in Ninja

Cooking Instructions:

1. Spray multi-purpose pan with cooking spray and set it aside.

2. Stir butter, brown sugar, egg, and vanilla in bowl. Now add your oats, flour, salt, and blueberries.

3. Stir until well combined, pour into pan next add your 2 cups water to your Ninja and set on rack.

4. Set oven at 400°F for about 40 to 45 minutes cover and cook till set in center and lightly browned at edges.

5. Serve immediately and Enjoy!

Bread Pudding

Preparation time: 5 minutes

Cooking time: 40 minutes

Overall time: 45 minutes

Serves: 2 to 4 people

Recipe Ingredients:

- 6 slices of day-old bread or cinnamon raisin bread (toasted)
- 4 eggs, beaten
- 2 cups of milk
- 2 tablespoons of butter or margarine, melted
- 1 teaspoon of cinnamon
- 1 teaspoon of vanilla extract
- ¾ cup of sugar
- ½ cup of raisins

Cooking Instructions:

1. Preheat on oven setting to 350°F. In a bowl break up the bread into small pieces and drizzle the melted butter over the bread and set it aside.

2. In another bowl, combine the remaining ingredients and mix well. Dump the bread and butter into the crock.

3. Pour the well mixed liquid over the bread until well saturated. Bake for about 45 minutes at 350°F or until the bread has a sponge-like consistency.

4. Serve immediately and Enjoy!

Brownies from Scratch

Preparation time: 5 minutes

Cooking time: 25 minutes

Overall time: 30 minutes

Serves: 3 to 5 people

Recipe Ingredients

- ¼ cup of oil
- 1 cup of white sugar
- 1 teaspoon of vanilla
- 2 eggs
- ½ cup of all-purpose flour
- 1/3 cup of cocoa powder
- ¼ teaspoon of baking powder
- ¼ teaspoon of salt
- ½ cup of chocolate chips

Cooking Instructions:

1. As you assemble your ingredients, add 3 cups of water to your Ninja & and turn to the Oven setting of 325°F.

2. Grease the multipurpose pan, in a medium mixing bowl, mix oil, sugar, & vanilla. Beat in eggs.

3. Combine flour, cocoa, baking powder, & salt in small bowl & gradually stir into mixture until blended.

4. Stir in chocolate chips then spread into pan. Place your rack and the pan. Bake for about 25 minutes.

5. Allow to cool before serving.

Cheesecake

Preparation time: 15 minutes

Cooking time: 55 minutes

Overall time: 1 hour 10 minutes

Serves: 8 to 10 people

Recipe Ingredients:

- ½ cup of graham cracker crumbs
- 2 tbsp. of melted butter
- 1 tbsp. of sugar
- ¼ cup of sugar
- 1½ (8 oz.) packages cream cheese (12 oz total), softened
- 2 eggs
- ½ cup of sour cream
- 1 tsp. of vanilla extract
- 4 cups of water
- 6-inch round pan

Cooking Instructions:

1. Stir graham cracker crumbs, butter, and 1 tablespoon of sugar in bowl, press mixture into bottom and sides of pan.

2. Use your fingers to beat cream cheese with ¼ cup sugar in bowl with electric mixer until smooth.

3. Beat in 1 whole egg and the whites from the second egg and 1 teaspoon of vanilla extract. Mix in ½ cup of sour cream and pour batter into prepared pan.

4. Pour 4 cups water into pot, place roasting rack into pot and place filled cake pan on rack and cover with lid.

5. Set Oven to 325°F for about 55 minutes. Do not lift lid during cooking. Check center of cake after 50 minutes.

6. turn the Ninja off if it is done, but If not, let it cook for 5 more minutes. Remove pan from pot, let cool.

7. Cover and refrigerate at least 4 hours or overnight. Top with favorite fruit topping and serve.

Coconut Blueberry Coffee

Preparation time: 10 minutes

Cooking time: 30 minutes

Overall time: 40 minutes

Serves: 2 to 4 people

Recipe Ingredients:

- 2 cups of flour
- 1 cup of sugar
- 3 tsp. of baking powder
- ¼ tsp. of salt
- 2 eggs
- 1 cup of milk
- ½ cup of oil
- 1½ cups of blueberries
- 1 cup of coconut

Cooking Instructions:

1. Preheat Ninja for about 10 minutes on the Oven temperature of 375°F while preparing mix.

2. Combine flour, sugar, baking powder and salt. In another bowl beat eggs, milk and oil; stir into dry ingredients until moistened.

3. Fold in blueberries and transfer to your multipurpose pan. Sprinkle with coconut. Place your rack in the Ninja and add your pan.

4. Cover with the lid and bake until toothpick inserted comes out clean. This took about 30 minutes. Cool on wire rack.

5. Serve immediately and Enjoy!

Angus Roast Beef

Preparation time: 5 minutes

Cooking time: 10 minutes

Overall time: 15 minutes

Serves: 2 to 4 people

Recipe Ingredients:

- 3½ pounds of angus roast beef
- Salt & pepper
- Worcestershire sauce
- 1 box of beef broth/stock
- ½ red onion, thin sliced
- Stalk of celery
- 3 redskin potatoes, quartered
- Mini carrots
- A handful of each fresh basil and flat leaf parsley
- Flour/water, for rue
- ½ cup of sangria

Cooking Instructions:

1. Generously salt & pepper roast and coat with Worcestershire sauce. Add the roast to your rack.

2. To the bottom of the Ninja pot, add beef broth, ½ of the red onion and a stalk of celery, and a couple shakes of Worcestershire to the broth.

3. Add your rack to the pot. Add the potatoes around roast, carrots and the remaining onions, top the roast with the basil and parsley. Cover.

4. Turn your Ninja to 350°F and bake until it's done as you prefer. Use a temperature probe to test. Adjust your time according to size.

5. Take the roast and veggies out and turn your Ninja to Stove Top High and make your rue with the broth, flour and water.

6. Add about ½ cup of Sangria. Cover and let it cook for about 5 minutes to thicken a little.

7. Serve immediately and Enjoy!

Bacon Cheeseburger Meatloaf

Preparation time: 5 minutes

Cooking time: 30 minutes

Overall time: 35 minutes

Serves: 2 to 4 people

Recipe Ingredients:

- 2 pounds of hamburger
- 2 cloves of finely minced garlic cloves
- 2 tablespoons of finely chopped onion
- 3 tablespoon of Worcestershire sauce
- 3-5 pieces of cooked crumbled bacon
- 1 cup of shredded cheese
- Salt and pepper to taste

Cooking Instructions:

1. Mix the above ingredients; form into a loaf

2. Set Ninja to Oven Setting of 350°F and place on rack. Set timer for about 30 minutes.

3. Serve immediately and Enjoy!

Barbacoa

Preparation time: 5 minutes

Cooking time: 6 hours

Overall time: 6 hour 5 minutes

Serves: 6 to 8 people

Recipe Ingredients:

- 5 pounds of chuck roast
- 1/3 cup of apple cider vinegar
- 4 tsp. of minced garlic cloves
- 4 tsp. of cumin
- 2 tsp. of oregano
- 1 tsp. of ground black pepper
- 1 tsp. of salt
- ½ tsp. of ground cloves
- 2 tbsp. of vegetable oil
- ¾ cup of chicken broth
- 3 bay leaves
- 3 tbsp. of lime juice
- 4 chipotle chiles in adobo

Cooking Instructions:

1. Combine vinegar, lime juice, chipotles, garlic, cumin, oregano, black pepper, salt and cloves in a blender or processor on high speed until smooth.

2. Remove most of the fat from the roast and then cut into large chunks. Turn the Ninja to Stove Top High.

3. Add the oil and sear all sides of the roast until browned, add the adobo sauce to the meat.

4. Add the chicken broth and add the bay leaves. Turn the Ninja to Slow Cook High for 6 hours or Slow Cook Low for 8 hours. Carefully shred the meat with two forks.

5. Turn the Ninja to Buffet/Warm setting. Serve with hard or soft tortilla shells when ready.

6. Typical sides include tortillas, rice, black or pinto beans, cheese, pico de gallo, guacamole, and sour cream.

Beef & Broccoli

Preparation time: 5 minutes

Cooking time: 6 hours

Overall time: 6 hours 5 minutes

Serves: 2 to 4 people

Recipe Ingredients:

- 1 lb. of boneless beef chuck roast, sliced into thin strips
- 1 cup of beef consommé
- ½ cup of soy sauce
- 1/3 cup of brown sugar
- 1 tbsp. of sesame oil
- 3 garlic cloves, minced
- 2 tbsp. of cornstarch
- 2 tbsp. of sauce from the crock pot after being cooked
- Fresh broccoli florets
- Hot cooked rice

Cooking Instructions:

1. Place beef in your Ninja, in a small bowl, combine consommé, soy sauce, brown sugar, oil, and garlic.

2. Pour over beef. Cook on low for about 8 hours. In a cup, stir cornstarch and sauce from the Ninja pot until smooth.

3. Add to the pot. Stir well to combine. Add broccoli to the Ninja pot. Stir to combine. Cover and cook an additional 30 minutes on high.

4. Serve over hot cooked rice.

Beef & Noodles

Preparation time: 15 minutes

Cooking time: 6 hours 30 minutes

Overall time: 5 hours 45 minutes

Serves: 4 to 6 people

Recipe Ingredients:

- Boneless ribs
- Lipton onion soup mix
- 1 teaspoon of Worchester sauce
- 1 cup of water
- 1 onion, chopped
- 2 cans of mushrooms
- 2 cans of beef gravy
- 1 bag (about 16 ounces) of egg noodles or shells
- 4½ cups of water

Cooking Instructions:

1. Place the ribs, onion soup, Worchester, and water in the Ninja and turn to Slow Cook Low for 6 hours.

2. Pull apart the rib meat. Add onion, mushrooms and gravy. Continue cooking on Slow Cook Low for 1-2 hours longer.

3. Add noodles or shells and water. Turn to Oven setting of 300°. Stir to mix. Cook for about 15 minutes and stir again.

4. After 30 minutes of cooking time, stir and turn to Buffet setting. Serve immediately and Enjoy!

Asian Pork Chops

Preparation time: 10 minutes

Cooking time: 2 hours

Overall time: 2 hours 10 minutes

Serves: 3 to 5 people

Recipe Ingredients:

- 1-inch thick cut pork chops
- 1 onion, sliced thick
- 2 garlic cloves, cubed
- A little amount of olive oil
- 16 ounces can of chicken broth
- ¼ cup of low sodium soy sauce
- ½ cup of ketchup
- ¼ cup of honey
- ¼ cup of brown sugar
- ¼ teaspoon of chili sauce
- Pinch ginger

Cooking Instructions:

1. Sauté pork chops in olive oil on Stove Top High.

2. Remove and add onion and garlic, soften. Add chicken broth and rest of ingredients. Stir and put the chops back in.

3. Turn to Slow Cook Low and cook 2 ½-3 hours. When chops are just done add 2 tablespoon of corn starch mixed with a little water.

4. Thicken sauce and serve with rice. You can also put the sauce on the rice as well.

Baby Back Ribs & Sausage

Preparation time: 5 minutes

Cooking time: 3 hours

Overall time: 3 hours 5 minutes

Serves: 2 to 4 people

Recipe Ingredients:

- 5 lbs. rack of meaty baby back ribs.

For a rub:

- 4 tbsp. of smoked paprika
- 4 tbsp. of brown sugar
- 3 tbsp. of chili powder
- 2 tbsp. of garlic powder
- 1 tbsp. of celery salt
- 1 tbsp. of dry mustard
- 2 cups of water for the Ninja pot
- 1 pound of smoked sausage of choice
- Barbeque sauce of choice

Cooking Instructions:

1. Mix all spices together or use your choice of dry rub. Rub into meat front and back.

2. Place rib haves in zip lock or place on platter/plate then cover with clear wrap and refrigerate overnight.

3. Place the water in the Ninja pot. Place the rack and add rubbed rib halves on the rack and place the lid.

4. Turn the Ninja to the Oven setting of 250°F and cook for about 3 hours. Remove the lid and place sausage pieces on sides of ribs.

5. Brush ribs and sausage with desired amount of Barbeque sauce. Replace the lid and cook an additional hour or until folk tender.

6. Line a baking sheet with aluminum foil and placed cooked ribs and sausage on and bushed with additional Barbeque sauce.

7. Place under the boiler of the regular oven a few minutes. Enjoy

Barbeque Pulled Pork

Preparation time: 5 minutes

Cooking time: 6 hours

Overall time: 6 hours 5 minutes

Serves: 4 to 6 people

Recipe Ingredients:

- 3 pounds of pork loin
- Salt & pepper, to taste
- 1 onion, chopped
- 3 garlic cloves, minced
- 1 teaspoon of smoked paprika
- 1 teaspoon of chili powder
- 1 teaspoon of dried mustard
- ½ teaspoon of cayenne pepper
- 1 cup of ketchup
- 1 tablespoon of tomato paste
- 2 tablespoons of brown sugar
- ¼ cup of apple cider
- 1 teaspoon of salt
- 1 cup of beef or chicken stock

Cooking Instructions:

1. Salt & pepper the pork, turn the Ninja to Stove Top High.

2. Add the oil to heat. When hot, add the pork and brown on all sides. Remove and set it aside.

3. Add the onion and garlic, cook a few minutes. Add dry spices, cook a few minutes. Add rest of ingredients and stir. Add pork.

4. With a spoon pull some of the sauce up on it. Turn to Slow Cook Low for 6 hours. Check for tenderness at 5-hours mark.

5. When pork is done it will shred easily with a fork. Shred the meat. Top with as much sauce as desired.

6. Serve on buns. It is easily frozen for later.

Beer Brats in Onion Gravy

Preparation time: 10 minutes

Cooking time: 30 minutes

Overall time: 40 minutes

Serves: 3 to 5 people

Recipe Ingredients:

- Brats
- Onions
- Olive oil
- 12 oz. of lite beer
- McCormick brown gravy mix
- ½ teaspoon of thyme

Cooking Instructions:

1. Turn your Ninja to Stove Top High and sauté the onions in olive oil and Remove.

2. In the oil remaining brown the brats for about 6-8 minutes turning so they were uniformly brown.

3. Pour 6 ounces of lite beer over the brats and cook on Stove Top Medium for about 12 minutes. Return the onions to the pot to cover the brats.

4. Make the gravy and add the thyme. Pour it into beer and brats and turn your Ninja to Stove Top Low to simmer for about 20 minutes or more.

5. Serve over noodles of choice with some fresh cucumber and sour cream/onions salad.

Brown Sugar & Balsamic Glazed Pork Loin

Preparation time: 5 minutes

Cooking time: 6 hours

Overall time: 6 hours 5 minutes

Serves: 4 to 6 people

Recipe Ingredients:

- 2 pound of boneless pork tenderloin
- Dry rub- 1 teaspoon of ground sage
- ½ teaspoon of salt
- ¼ teaspoon of pepper
- 1 clove of garlic crushed
- Glaze- ½ cup of brown sugar
- 1 tablespoon of cornstarch
- ¼ cup of balsamic vinegar
- ½ cup of water
- 2 tablespoon of soy sauce

Cooking Instructions:

1. Mix all dry rub ingredients and rub into tenderloin. Put ½ cup of water in Ninja and add the tenderloin.

2. Cook on low for 6 hours. About 1 hour before tenderloin is done combine the Glaze ingredients in a saucepan and heat until thick.

3. Pour on tenderloin 3 times during last hour of cooking. Serve with the sauce.

Lamb & Onions

Preparation time: 5 minutes

Cooking time: 4 hours

Overall time: 4 hours 5 minutes

Serves: 2 to 4 people

Recipe Ingredients:

- 2 pieces of lamb shoulder
- 2 onions, sliced
- 4 cloves of garlic, chopped
- 1 can of chicken broth
- Salt and pepper to taste
- 2 tablespoons of butter
- 1 tablespoon of olive oil
- Flour to coat

Cooking Instructions:

1. Season lamb with salt and pepper, lightly flour.

2. Add butter and olive oil to your Ninja. Brown lamb on Stove Top High and add the onions, garlic and chicken broth.

3. Turn to Slow Cook Low for 4 hours or until tender. Serve over wide egg noodles

Crustless Low Carb Pumpkin Pie

Preparation time: 10 minutes

Cooking time: 30 minutes

Overall time: 40 minutes

Serves: 2 to 4 people

Recipe Ingredients:

- 1 can (15 oz.) of pumpkin
- ½ cup of milk
- 4 large eggs, beaten
- 2 teaspoons of vanilla
- ¼ cup of Splenda
- ½ teaspoon of salt
- 2 teaspoon pumpkin pie spice
- Pecans, chopped – for topping
- Reddi Whip or fat-free or low-fat frozen whipped topping, thawed

Cooking Instructions:

1. Turn the Ninja to 350°F and preheat for about 10 minutes.

2. Spray your multi-purpose pan with oil or a nonstick cooking spray. In a large bowl, combine the pumpkin, eggs, milk, vanilla, sweetener and spices.

3. Spread the mixture evenly in the pan. You will be steam baking. Add 2 cups of water to the pot. Place the Ninja rack with multi-purpose pan in the pot.

4. Bake for 30 minutes or until a knife inserted into the center comes out clean. Serve immediately and Enjoy!

Rack of Lamb with Potatoes & Onions

Preparation time: 5 minutes

Cooking time: 30 minutes

Overall time: 35 minutes

Serves: 3 to 5 people

Recipe Ingredients:

- 1 rack of lamb
- Salt & pepper - to taste
- 2 tablespoons of butter
- 2 tablespoons of olive oil
- Garlic & rosemary – to taste
- 2 large whole onions
- 1½ cups of beef stock
- 4 potatoes
- Garlic, thyme, olive oil, salt & pepper – for potatoes
- Pyramid mat – trimmed to fit

Cooking Instructions:

1. Season Rack of Lamb with salt & pepper.

2. Turn the Ninja to Stove Top High. Add butter, olive oil, garlic and rosemary to your Ninja pot & sear lamb on all sides.

3. Sear the onions until brown on both sides and add the beef stock to the pot. Place the trimmed Pyramid Mat on ½ of the bottom of the pot.

4. Add the seasoned potatoes on top of mat. Place the Rack of Lamb meat side down on top and place the lid.

5. Turn Ninja to Bake/Oven, with a temperature of 400°F and leave for about 30 Minutes.

6. Check and add more beef stock if needed while lamb is baking, or onions might burn. Remove lamb and cover in foil.

7. Check potatoes and leave in if they need more time while the lamb is resting in foil. Serve immediately and Enjoy!

Roast Lamb Gyros

Preparation time: 5 minutes

Cooking time: 10 minutes

Overall time: 15 minutes

Serves: 2 to 4 people

Recipe Ingredients:

Couscous:

- ½ red onion, diced
- 1 bell pepper, diced
- 2 cloves of garlic, minced
- ½ cup of dry couscous
- 1 cup of stock
- ½ cup water
- 1 teaspoon of butter
- 1 teaspoon of oil

Gyros:

- Pita breads or flat breads
- Dry coleslaw
- ¼ cup of Greek yogurt
- 1 tablespoon of mint sauce
- Left over roast lamb cup into strips
- Seasoning of choice
- Feta cheese, cubed

Cooking Instructions:

1. On Stove Top Low melt the butter and add oil. Fry the onions, bell pepper and garlic until onions are translucent.

2. Add the couscous and stir, toasting for about 3 minutes. Take the pot out of the cooker so the water you add later doesn't boil away.

3. Turn the Ninja off and put the lamb on the roasting rack and season as you wish. Place the pot back in the cooker.

4. Add in the stock and then quickly place the rack into the pot and cover. Turn the Ninja to the Oven setting of 300°F, for about 5 minutes.

5. While it's cooking put the pitas in the toaster. Stir the yogurt, mint sauce and feta through the coleslaw.

6. Once the 5 minutes are up, check to see if the couscous is done or if it needs more water.

7. If so, add half a cup more water and turn the Ninja to Stove Top Low to allow it to boil away.

8. While it boils build your gyros by stuffing the pitas with the coleslaw and lamb. Serve with the cooked couscous.

Rice & Pasta Recipes

Chicken Ravioli

Preparation time: 15 minutes

Cooking time: 25 minutes overall

time: 40 minutes

Serves: 2 to 4 people

Recipe Ingredients:

- 1 bag of refrigerated chicken ravioli
- 24 oz. jar of marinara
- ½ cup of water
- A few dollops of ricotta cheese and some mozzarella

Cooking Instructions:

1. Add all of the ingredients, except cheesed and stir continuously until the ingredients are well mixed together.

2. Turn your Ninja to the Oven setting of 250°F for 15 minutes. After the 15 minutes, add the cheeses and cook for 10 more minutes, or until tender.

3. Serve immediately and enjoy!

Chicken & Rice Bake

Preparation time: 15 minutes

Cooking time: 45 minutes

Total time: 60 minutes Serves: 2

to 8 people

Recipe Ingredients:

- 2 large chicken breasts cut in half
- 2 cups of white rice
- 1 box of chicken broth
- 1 bag of frozen broccoli and cauliflower
- Salt, pepper and paprika to taste

Cooking Directions:

1. Set your Ninja to oven mode of 350°F. Add rice, stock, chicken and veggies in the Ninja.

2. After that, add plenty of paprika and a bit of salt and pepper. Cook for about 45 minutes or until rice is tender.

3. Serve immediately and enjoy hot.

Chicken & Rice Casserole

Preparation time: 10 minutes

Cooking time: 25 minutes

Gross time: 35 minutes

Serves: 2 to 8 people

Recipe Ingredients:

- 2 tbsp. of unsalted butter
- 2 cloves of garlic, finely chopped
- 4 scallions, sliced
- 2 cups of broccoli florets
- 2 cups of shredded rotisserie chicken (skin removed)
- 1 cup of medium-grain white rice
- 1 plum of tomato, chopped
- Kosher salt and freshly ground pepper
- 2 cups of low-sodium chicken broth
- ¼ cup of sour cream
- 1 cup of diced dill havarti cheese (about 4 oz.)
- ¼ cup of grated parmesan cheese (about 1 oz.)

Cooking Instructions:

1. Select the Sear/Sauté function on your Ninja, set your Ninja on Stove Top High and Sauté the garlic and onions.

2. Add the rest of your ingredients and switch your Ninja to Oven Mode at 425°F for 20 minutes.

3. Sprinkle with the remaining havarti and parmesan, then broil about 2 minutes until it turns golden completely.

4. Then Sprinkle with the reserved scallions. Now serve and enjoy your delicious meal hot!

Alfredo Three Cheese Bow Tie Chicken

Preparation time: 20 minutes

Cooking time: 30 minutes

Gross time: 50 minutes

Serve: 2 to 4 people

Recipe Ingredients:

- 14 ounces of jars Prego 3 Artisan Alfredo sauce
- 4 boneless, skinless chicken breast, cut in cubes
- ½ cup of green peas
- ½ cup of yellow corn
- ½ tbsp. of real bacon bits
- 4 cups of chicken broth
- 1 pounds of bow tie pasta

Cooking Instructions:

1. Set your Ninja to Stove mode and set at Top High pressure to brown your chicken cubes.

2. Add remaining ingredients to Chicken. Turn to the Oven setting of 300°F for 30 minutes, or until pasta is tender.

3. Serve immediately and enjoy!

Aunt Jill's Cheese Grits

Preparation time: 7 minutes

Cooking time: 25 minutes

Overall time: 32 minutes

Serves: 2 to 4 people

Recipe Ingredients:

- 2 cups of water
- 1¼ cups of milk
- 1 tsp. of salt
- 1 cup of quick cooking grits
- ½ cup of plus 1 tbsp. butter
- 1/3 cup of diced green onions
- 4 ounces of processed cheddar cheese, cubed (Velveeta)
- ¼ tsp. of garlic powder
- 2½ cups of shredded cheddar cheese
- (10-ounces) can diced tomatoes and green chilies with liquid (Ro-Tel)

Cooking Instructions:

1. Select Sear/Sauté on your Ninja and Sauté green onions in 1 tablespoon butter for a minute or so.

2. Now add remaining ingredients, reserving ½ cup cheddar. After that, cook at 350°F for 25 minutes, stirring occasionally.

3. Sprinkle reserved cheddar on top, close lid for a few minutes until the cheese melts.

4. Wow! Cheese is ready, serve and enjoy.

Baked Pasta

Preparation time: 15 minutes

Cooking time: 45

Total time: 60 minutes Serves: 2

to 8 people

Recipe Ingredients:

- 1 lb. of ground beef or sausage browned & drained of fat
- Sliced pepperoni
- 4 cups of shredded mozzarella cheese or any blend you like
- 16 oz. bag of egg noodles cooked & drained as package directs
- 24 oz. of your favourite tomato sauce
- Italian seasonings

Cooking Instructions:

1. Serve 1/3 of the sauce on the bottom of your Ninja, top with noodles (we always stir up this 1st layer of noodles & sauce).

2. Top it with 1/3 of the browned meat. Top again with 1/3 of the cheese & sliced pepperoni & sprinkle on a dash of the seasoning.

3. Repeat layers 2 more times, then set your Ninja to Slow Cook High for about 45 minutes.

4. Now serve hot and enjoy.

Basil Parmesan Chicken, Broccoli & Rice Bake

Preparation time: 20 minutes

Cooking time: 40 minutes

Total time: 60 minutes Serves: 2

to 4 people

Recipe Ingredients:

- 2 large chicken breasts cut in half for 4 servings
- Steak seasoning
- 14 ounces of bag frozen broccoli
- 1 1/3 cups of rice
- 1 can of Progresso Recipe Starter Basil Parmesan
- 1½ cans of water (use the Progresso can)
- ½ cup of shredded cheese of choice to sprinkle on top

Cooking Instructions:

1. Put rice in the pot and stir in the Progresso starter and add 2 cans of water. Add the frozen broccoli and stir adequately.

2. Season chicken breasts with steak seasoning and add to the pot. Set your Ninja on Oven 350°F and cook for about 40 minutes

3. Turn the Ninja off, add the cheese to the top, and return the lid until its ready to eat.

4. Serve and enjoy immediately!

Basil-Tomato Pasta

Preparation time: 10 minutes

Cooking time: 30 minutes

Gross time: 40 minutes

Serve: 2 to 4 people

Recipe Ingredients:

- 12 ounces of linguine pasta
- 15 ounces of can dice tomatoes
- 1 large sweet onion, julienned
- 4 cloves of garlic, thinly sliced
- ½ teaspoon of red pepper flakes
- 2 teaspoons of dried oregano leaves
- 2 large strips of fresh basil chopped
- 4 cups of vegetable broth, plus ½ cup water
- 2 tablespoons of olive oil
- Salt and pepper (to taste)
- Parmesan cheese, for garnish

Cooking Instructions:

1. In the Ninja pot, place pasta, tomatoes, onion, garlic, and basil.

2. Pour in broth and water. Sprinkle the pepper flakes and oregano on top then drizzle with olive oil.

3. Turn Ninja to the Oven setting of 300°F, for 30 minutes. Stir every 5 minutes. A spaghetti serving spoon does well, lifting and stirring gently.

4. Season to taste with salt and pepper. Garnish with Parmesan cheese. It also good with some cooked shrimp, garlic bread.

5. Serve immediately and enjoy!

Beef & Cheese- Better than Hamburger Helper

Preparation time: 10 minutes

Cooking time: 14 minutes

Total time: 24 minutes

Serves: 2 to 4 people

Recipe Ingredients:

- 1 lb. of ground beef
- 1 box of Kraft mac & cheese
- 2 cups of water
- ¼ cup of butter, ¼ cup milk and cheese packet
- Seasonings of preference

Cooking Instructions:

1. Turn the Ninja to Stove Top High. Brown the ground beef. Remove and drain excess grease. Set aside and wipe the Ninja.

2. Add the water and macaroni. Carefully place the lid and turn to 250°F. Set time on Ninja for 10 minutes.

3. Take off the lid and stir for 4 minutes. After Water is evaporated, take the pot out of the Ninja to stop the cooking

4. Now add the beef and season as desired. Add your ¼ cup butter, ¼ cup milk and cheese packet, stir until well mixed.

5. Serve immediately and enjoy.

Beef Nacho Casserole

Preparation time: 10 minutes

Cooking time: 10 minutes

Overall time: 20 minutes

Serves: 2 to 4 people

Recipe Ingredient:

- 1 lb. of ground beef
- 1 can of black beans (drained & rinsed)
- 1 can of sliced black olives (drained)
- 1 to 8 oz. can of tomato sauce
- ¼ cup of salsa
- ¼ tsp. each of garlic salt, cumin & onion powder
- 1 to 2 cups of shredded cheese
- Crushed tortilla chips

Cooking Instructions:

1. Turn your Ninja to Stove mode, select pressure function and set to High pressure to brown the ground beef.

2. Drain any excess grease then turn Ninja to Stove mode and set to cook at Low pressure.

3. Add the tomato sauce and seasonings, let simmer for a few minutes. Add the salsa, beans and olives, top with cheese and tortilla chips.

4. Then turn your Ninja to the Oven setting of 300°F, allow to bake for about 10 minutes.

KETOGENIC RECIPES

Baked Garlic Chicken Thighs

Preparation time: 10 minutes

Cooking time: 45 minutes

Overall time: 55 minutes

Serves: 6 to 8 people

Recipe Ingredients:

- ½ cup of butter
- 3 tbsp. of minced garlic
- 3 tbsp. of low sodium soy sauce
- ¼ tsp. of black pepper
- 1 tbsp. of dried rosemary
- 10 chicken thighs

Cooking Instructions:

1. Turn your Ninja to 400° and preheat about 10 minutes. Lightly grease the Ninja pot.

2. In a microwave safe bowl, mix the butter, garlic, soy sauce, pepper, and rosemary. Cook on High in the microwave, until butter is melted.

3. Arrange chicken in the Ninja pot and brush with the butter mixture, reserving some of the mixture for basting.

4. Bake the chicken for about 25 minutes. Turn chicken over. Baste with remaining butter mixture.

5. Bake for an additional 20 minutes or until juices run clear. Serve immediately and Enjoy!

Beef, Sausage & Cauliflower Bake

Preparation time: 10 minutes

Cooking time: 20 minutes

Overall time: 30 minutes

Serves: 3 to 5 people

Recipe Ingredients:

- 1 large head cauliflower
- 1 pound of lean ground beef
- 1 pound of ground sausage
- 2 cans of cream of celery soup
- 1 cup of milk
- ½ cup of Parmesan cheese
- Shredded cheese for the top
- Salt and pepper
- Chopped garlic

Cooking Instructions:

1. Cut up the cauliflower and steam in the Ninja for about 15 minutes.

2. Once the cauliflower is steamed clean out the Ninja and cook the beef, sausage and garlic on Stove Top High until meat is browned.

3. Add a little salt no pepper. Drain. In a bowl, combine soup, milk and Parmesan cheese.

4. Add the cauliflower to the meat mixture and stir, pour soup mixture over all. Turn the Oven to 325°F. for about 15 minutes.

5. Turn the Ninja off. Stir everything together and top with shredded cheese and cover for 5 more minutes or until cheese is melted.

6. Serve immediately and Enjoy!

Cheese Steak Stuffed Green Peppers

Preparation time: 5 minutes

Cooking time: 20 minutes

Overall time: 25 minutes

Serves: 2 to 4 people

Recipe Ingredients:

- 2 large green peppers - cut in half; stem to bottom
- 4 large white button mushrooms - chopped
- 1 medium yellow onion - chopped
- 1½ pound of shaved steak
- 1½ cups of spaghetti or marina sauce (We like Newman's)
- 8-ounce bag of mozzarella cheese
- Garlic powder - to taste
- Salt & pepper - to taste

Cooking Instructions:

1. Sauté onions and mushrooms in Ninja on Stove Top High.

2. Add shaved steak and seasonings. Once the meat is browned, remove from the Ninja.

3. Fill each half of the pepper with meat and add a little sauce in each. Add the remaining cup of sauce to the bottom of the Ninja.

4. Arrange the amount of cheese you like. Turn to the Oven setting of 250°F for about 20 minutes. You will be softening the pepper and melting the cheese.

5. Serve over brown or white rice.

Chicken Pizza

Preparation time: 10 minutes

Cooking time: 3 hours

Overall time: 3 hours 10 minutes

Serves: 4 to 6 people

Recipe Ingredients:

- 2 large boneless, skinless chicken breasts cut into cubes
- ½ tsp. of salt
- 1/8 tsp. of pepper
- 1 tsp. of dried Italian seasoning
- 1 purple onion, chopped
- 3 cloves of garlic, minced
- 2 bell peppers, cut into 1" pieces
- 14 ounces of jar of pizza sauce
- ¼ cup of water
- ½ can of sliced black olives
- 2 ounces of sliced pepperoni, optional
- 1 cup of shredded pizza cheese

Cooking Instructions:

1. Brown chicken chunks, onion, green peppers in bottom of Ninja.

2. Pour juices off and add pepperoni and olives. Mix seasoning and water well into pizza sauce.

3. Pour over chicken, pepperoni, olives, onion, green pepper. Turn your Ninja to Slow Cook Low for about 3 hours.

4. Turn Ninja off. Spread cheese over chicken mixture. Put lid on and let stand for about 10 minutes before serving.

Green Chile Chicken Enchilada Casserole

Preparation time: 10 minutes

Cooking time: 5 hours

Overall time: 5 hours 10 minutes

Serves: 4 to 6 people

Recipe Ingredients:

- 1 pound of boneless skinless chicken breast
- 1 large can of green enchilada sauce
- 1 can of sliced olives
- 1 can of diced green chiles
- 2 cups of shredded cheese
- 6 low carb flour tortillas
- hot sauce
- 15 ounces of chicken stock

Cooking Instructions:

1. Add the chicken and stock to the Ninja pot. Turn to Slow Cook Low for 5 hours. When cooked through, remove juices and chicken.

2. Shred the chicken. Add the shredded chicken to a bowl with the olives, chilies and hot sauce.

3. Stir and add a little enchilada sauce to the Ninja pot. Place 2 tortillas over the sauce, Add some meat mixture and cheese.

4. Repeat the process for 2 more layers. Add the rest of the green sauce to the Ninja. Turn your Ninja to Slow Cook High for an hour.

5. Serves immediately and Enjoy!

Zucchini Casserole

Preparation time: 5 minutes

Cooking time: 15 minutes

Overall time: 20 minutes

Serves: 2 to 4 people

Recipe Ingredients:

- 1½ pounds of zucchini
- 1 small onion
- 2 tablespoons of butter
- 1 cup (4 ounces) of diced green chilies
- 3 tablespoons of flour
- ½ teaspoon of salt
- ¼ teaspoon of pepper
- 1½ cups of jack cheese
- 1 egg
- 1 cup of small curd cottage cheese
- 2 tablespoons of minced parsley
- ½ cup of grated parmesan cheese

Cooking Instructions:

1. Dice zucchini, combine with onion & butter in Ninja on Stove Top Medium.

2. Sauté and mix in drained chilies, flour, salt & Pepper. Sprinkle with jack cheese. Mix egg with cottage cheese & parsley and spoon over the top.

3. Sprinkle with parmesan cheese. Bake at 300° for 20 minutes, or until hot in the center.

Meatballs with Spinach, Mushrooms & Sauce

Preparation time: 5 minutes

Cooking time: 3 hours

Overall time: 3 hours 5 minutes

Serves: 3 to 5 people

Recipe Ingredients:

- 10 ounces of chopped spinach
- 16 ounces of meatballs
- 24 ounces of jar sauce
- 2 tablespoons of minced garlic
- 8 ounces of sliced mushrooms
- ½ cup of diced onion
- 1 tablespoon of olive oil
- Angel pasta - optional
- Parmesan cheese for topping

Cooking Instructions:

1. Turn the Ninja to Stove Top High. Heat the olive oil.

2. Add the meatballs to brown and the onions and mushrooms to sauté. When done, add the sauce and spinach.

3. Turn to Slow Cook Low for 3 hours. Stirring a couple of times. serve with your favorite pasta.

Lentil Soup with Italian Sausage

Preparation time: 10 minutes

Cooking time: 4 hours

Overall time: 4 hours 10 minutes

Serves: 3 to 4 people

Recipe Ingredients:

- 1 pounds of Italian sausage, remove from casing or slice
- 2 teaspoons of olive oil (or more, depending on your pan)
- 1 onion, diced into small pieces
- 3 cloves of garlic, minced
- 1 cup of dried brown lentils
- 8 cups of homemade chicken stock (or 3 to 4 cans broth plus a little water)
- 2 teaspoons of ground fennel (do not leave out)
- 2 teaspoons of dried thyme
- 2 teaspoons of rubbed sage (dried)
- Dash of crushed red pepper, if desired
- Salt and pepper
- 12 ounces of jar roasted red pepper
- 1 medium zucchini, diced

Cooking Instructions:

1. Heat olive oil in Ninja on Stove Top High, add Italian sausage and brown well, breaking sausage into pieces as it cooks.

2. Remove sausage. In same pan, adding more oil if needed, brown onions until softened and barely starting to brown, add garlic and sauté for a minute.

3. Switch to Slow Cook Low and add broth, sausage, lentils, and herbs. Cook on Slow Cook Low for about 3 hours, lentils will be soft.

4. Drain red pepper, then chop peppers, zucchini and kale. Add veggies to soup and cook for about 1 hour more.

5. Cook until some lentils are starting to fall apart and all flavors are well blended. Season with salt and fresh ground black pepper and serve hot.

Acknowledgement

In preparing the "Ninja Foodi Cookbook Beginners", I sincerely wish to acknowledge my indebtedness to my husband for his support and the wholehearted cooperation and vast experience of my two colleagues - Mrs. Alexandra bryne, and Mrs. Catherine Long.

Carol Newman

Lightning Source UK Ltd.
Milton Keynes UK
UKHW050947120721
387032UK00005B/37